What People Are Saying About *Eddie and Me*:

"Eddie and Me tak~~ ~~ ~~ ~~ ~~ ~~ ~~ ~~ ~~ ~~ ourney with unexpected twists a  h, ache and wonder, as a young l ı about life together." - Deepak

"Eight-year-old Eddie and his sixty-year-old buddy, Mr. Cooperman, make a wonderful story, and remind us of how important a father—or the absence of one—can be to a child." - Lamar Alexander, Former U.S. Secretary of Education and present U.S. Senator

"Eddie and Me is an endearing account of a beautiful relationship between two people from different worlds. Saul Cooperman has given deeply of himself so that Eddie might have new hope and a new vision for his life. This is a love story that will touch your heart and soul." - George H. Gallup, Jr., Chairman, The George H. Gallup International Institute

"Eddie and Me is a touching story of hope and joy finding common ground." - Bill Bradley, Former U.S. Senator, Presidential candidate, and Pro Basketball Hall of Fame player

"I hope that millions of people will read about your experiences with Eddie and step up to make a positive difference in the lives of children." - Lynn Swann, All-Pro, National Football Hall of Fame, former chairman of Big Brothers, Big Sisters

Eddie and Me

A STORY OF FRIENDSHIP

SAUL COOPERMAN

IPG

Intermedia Publishing Group

Eddie and Me

A Story of Friendship

Published by:
Intermedia Publishing Group, Inc.
P.O. Box 2825
Peoria, Arizona 85380
www.intermediapub.com

ISBN 978-1-935529-70-5

Eddie and Me is dedicated to:

Barbara Harris, who set a wonderful example for her boys, George Gallup Jr., whose enthusiasm got me to sit and begin to write, and Ray Chambers, who helped me understand the power of mentoring.

TABLE OF CONTENTS

FOREWORD

Few books have touched my heart and inspired me as much as Saul Cooperman's book, *Eddie and Me*. It is the story of Saul's fourteen-year mentoring relationship with an inner city African American youngster named Eddie.

Saul Cooperman is a former New Jersey Commissioner of Education and the founder of the 10,000 Mentors Program. Week after week, and year after year through friendship, tough love and persistence, Saul nurtured Eddie into sturdy manhood with far better prospects for the future than he would otherwise have had.

This book is not a manual on mentoring – a list of "do's" and "don'ts" – but a chronicle of weekly encounters between Saul and Eddie that reveal both the major challenges and the great rewards of mentoring. Writing in a clear style, Saul captures the dialogue between the two in a way that makes the book a lively and compelling read.

The reader gets a glimpse into Eddie's world, a world with which most people are unfamiliar. Eddie's horizons are limited to his neighborhood. All around him is violence, and he doesn't expect to live past seventeen. He is convinced that all whites hate black people. He lives a day to day existence and cannot picture a future for himself. His absentee father, "let him down," said Eddie.

Saul opened up Eddie's world in a wonderful way; taking him to ballgames, to the New Jersey shore, to New York City, the library at Rutgers University, and to Newark Liberty Airport where Eddie insisted that Saul go up and down with him on the escalator time after time. Mentoring is tough and demanding work, but Saul clearly had a lot of fun along the way. Shooting basketballs was one of the many pleasures they shared.

Ever the educator, Saul was always alert to "teaching moments", and helped Eddie learn about life skills. Saul stood by Eddie as he struggled with math and reading, reminding him that a good education is essential to having a good job later in life. Through role modeling and directed conversation, Saul helped Eddie develop positive character traits, such as tolerance and compassion, and brought out the innate goodness in his young sidekick.

Saul and Eddie had long, leisurely talks on many topics on a park bench, at McDonald's, and strolling through the woods with Saul listening as much as instructing. Saul was, in effect, being the good father that Eddie never had.

Saul and his late wife, Paulette, who played a key role in the mentoring process, opened up their home to Eddie. So limited was Eddie's world that in his first visit to the Cooperman home he was surprised to see that the house had *two* bathrooms. At one point in his visit he looked through the windows and asked, "Arc there any tigers out there in the woods?"

After a lot of bumps along the road, with Eddie even dropping out of school for a brief period, the young man ended up strong at age twenty-one, doing well in college, with a good part- time job and a girlfriend with good values. And Saul was satisfied that Eddie had a strong character and a charitable heart.

Saul learned from his intense fourteen-year-experience just how difficult it is for an inner city child without a father to become a productive, caring adult. He writes, "There needs to be someone in a young person's life who can fan the flame of hope and idealism."

Saul fervently hopes that an ever-increasing number of Americans will be drawn to mentoring. But, he cautions mentors not to take the responsibility lightly. "Persistence is the key." But, the rewards are great, and Saul writes: "From the bottom of my heart, if you hang in there, you will get much more than you give."

Serving on boards, writing checks, raising money for various causes, are all vitally important to help break down the wall between the privileged and the underprivileged – the "haves" and "have nots." Yet, one could maintain, the ultimate answer lies in mentoring; in hands-on, face to face, one-on-one encounters on a regular basis.

Mentoring can also have a powerful "ripple effect" on families, extended families and on neighborhoods. These vital encounters will long be remembered. Indeed in the years to come, there undoubtedly will be those who will recall the time when a tall white man from the suburbs named Saul cared enough to reach out to a frightened and vulnerable eight-year-old boy from the inner city of Newark, and to open up to him a whole new world of hope and exciting possibilities.

George Gallup, Jr. Founding Chairman
The George H. Gallup International Institute

INTRODUCTION

Many years before I decided to write about Eddie and me, I'd spoken publicly about our developing relationship. In fact, I'd already given a talk about Eddie and me to a conference where education, business, and civic leaders gathered.

That was back in 1997. The meeting was in Princeton, New Jersey and the hundred or so guests were invited by the Gallup International Foundation. George Gallup, Jr. had asked me to make some remarks about my work in Newark, New Jersey, trying to help families in that city.

I could have spoken about raising funds, trying to get some families off drug dependency and getting them into work-training programs, but that story had been told many, many times by people with more experience than I. I thought about talking about some success stories and also some failures, but I ended up deciding I would share some parts of my relationship with Eddie.

I started slowly enough, with a few anecdotes about our first exchanges, and related parts of the stories I will be sharing with you. I asked, "Why do we have so many children like this who grow up in poverty? Why does a nation as wealthy, stable and idealistic as ours go on year after year with so many kids starting the game of life with two strikes against them?"

I let the question hang there a while to look over the audience for a moment or two and let the silence fill the room.

A kid who's raised with these odds against him becomes disillusioned at a young age, like a boy a teacher told me about recently. She'd asked her fourth graders to write a brief composition about their heroes. Many kids might write about their favorite uncle or their dad or even a ball player who stopped long enough to autograph a ball. But there are others who are more like a nine year old she knew, who handed in these words after his teacher's request to talk about a hero.

> "I don't have no hero. When I almost died nobody never saved me. When I got hit by a car nobody grabed me.
>
> When I fell on my neck nobody helped me. When I almost got shot nobody told me to look out a built come in at your head. I had to due my self. I don't have no hero."

"This was written by someone," I explained to the audience, "who can't bring himself to hope and trust in the way most kids should be able to. This was written by someone who clearly has given up on the notion of heroes."

The first thing I wanted to emphasize to the audience was what I was trying to do in my relationship with Eddie. Without someone who can fan the flames of hope and idealism, it's easy for kids who are disadvantaged to give up on themselves, on their schools, on everything. Without the structure and emotional support systems in place, it's very simple for a child often to become disillusioned, cynical, and hard-hearted.

"And there are thousands of children like this," I noted to my audience. "And they are there now and will grow up gravitating to a life of inadequate skills, and little enthusiasm. What we will wind up with are millions of ill-prepared people who will not be able to be full-time participating citizens in our great country."

From the looks in the eyes of several people in the audience, I could tell my words were having some effect. One man squirmed a bit in his seat and some stopped looking at me and looked away uncomfortably.

I continued, "Most of us in this room are educated, well-off, not likely to ever go to prison. Think how different it is for young black men in our nation's population. The numbers here are astounding. The Sentencing Project in Washington, D.C. reported in its research that one out of every three young African American men between the ages of eighteen and thirty are either in jail, on parole, or awaiting trial. These numbers are staggering to comprehend."

I then explained that my choice for getting involved with Eddie, while he's still a boy, comes out of my personal reflections on matters such as these. I remember when I was a kid, going to religious school, I learned that if you save one person, it's as if you save the world.

The audience asked me many questions and people kept talking to me at lunch about why I should write about my relationship with Eddie. George Gallup, Jr. said, "You should write about your experiences. Others who might be thinking of making a commitment would like to know what you are doing and learning."

So, it was the result of the talk at the seminar that started me thinking about telling our story. Perhaps, as George said, it might be helpful to others who wish to work with and mentor a young child.

I am hopeful that years from now Eddie will have graduated high school, have a good job, and see a fuller world than the one he has now. I want to be part of his world when he is in his twenties.

But, what really moved me to think seriously about this happened a few years later when Eddie, who knew that I had written another book, said to me, "Mr. Cooperman, maybe you could write about us. Maybe people would read about us and then Tyrone and Jamal could get mentors, too. They want a mentor but can't get one."

"I've been thinking about this, too, Eddie. A man I like very much suggested I write about you and me. Let's see how things go and maybe we'll discuss this again."

"But, if you write a book you wouldn't use my real name would you?"

"Not if you don't want me to."

"What would you call me, if you didn't use my name?"

"I don't know. I'd have to think about it."

And that's when I began to look at what I had written in my diary about Eddie and me.

****

When I read my comments in my diary, I saw that there was a jumping from subject to subject when I would see Eddie. Sometimes we would talk about his neighborhood, his fatalistic outlook as a child, or frequent discussions about race. And, as I read, I had to smile at my persistence to pound education into Eddie's head.

I decided to write this book taking incidents and conversations from our meetings, meeting by meeting; the progress, the lack of progress, and the slow but sure building of trust and respect, chapter by chapter. Although the quotes aren't exact, they represent the essence of our conversations at that time.

SETTING THE STAGE

Eddie and I met in the summer of 1995. Eddie lives in Newark, New Jersey, about one mile from where I was born. On one hand our relationship is about friendship; it's also about my struggle to help raise Eddie to be a caring, self-sufficient person, ready to meet the challenges he must face as he grows toward adulthood. Challenges of poverty, drugs, violence, and low expectations. The challenge of a collective mindset that says, "I can't" rather than "I can."

Our friendship may seem a little strange because it does not look like we have a lot in common. As I said, I met Eddie when he was eight and I was sixty. So our age difference might seem to be an obvious handicap. By American standards, Eddie is poor. I'm not. I'm white. Eddie is black. Our friendship has grown slowly during the first year, and continues to grow stronger. We are genuinely fond of each other and our relationship resembles that of a favorite nephew and his best uncle. If someone took our picture, it might even make you laugh to see two such unlikely people visiting an airport, eating at McDonald's, or sitting together at a NETS game.

The simple part of our story is that what is different about us doesn't seem to matter. Anybody looking at us could figure that out in a second. They could also figure out, pretty fast, that their opinion would not keep us from enjoying what we were doing. Unexpected sights cause some people to ponder, if only for a second; seeing Catholic nuns, in their old fashioned habits, eating hot dogs at Yankee Stadium or observing disabled children, splashing around and laughing in a pool ringed with the wheelchairs in which these kids quietly spend so much of their time.

That's often the way it was with Eddie and me when people saw an old white man and a very young black boy together.

When I was first matched with Eddie, he was with his mom, Celie. I remember I asked why she wanted a mentor for her son and she said she wanted someone to help "raise her boy the right way". I asked if it wouldn't be better to match Eddie with an African American man, because they would have more in common. She said, "It doesn't make any difference to me if it doesn't to you. I just want him to learn the right thing to do."

So, this is a story about friendship and struggle, about the things that have happened to us over the course of fourteen years. Many more knowledgeable people than I have written about the larger social issues facing children in a tough urban setting so I won't write about those. I will, however, talk about Eddie's environment, which often conditions his approach to life, and his thoughts about "the future".

Within this context, there is sometimes tension between us as I attempt to "raise Eddie the right way", a way that often contrasts with what he sees as normal.

Although I was born in Newark in 1934, I spent almost all of my formative years in West Orange, New Jersey. I lived in a small three-bedroom home with my father, mother, and younger sister. We lived across from the "cow pastures," a part of West Orange that was changing from rural to suburban.

My dad was a salesman. Mom was a homemaker. They cared very much for my sister and me. They loved us while trying their best to provide us with what children need without spoiling us. The Cooperman's of West Orange can be described as a typical American family of the forties and fifties.

All the lessons were clearly in place for us as we grew up. When it came to play we were expected to be fair and always respect the opposition. We were also expected to use our abilities to the maximum, which meant we played hard. Being honest was something we learned and took for granted; it was the only thing you could be. Teachers and neighbors reinforced these and other values such as keeping our promises, respect for the property of others, and making a sincere effort. (I can still hear people saying, "Try again, Saul".) These values were imbued in us at so young an age that I cannot recall a time when their legitimacy was ever questioned. We were taught from the start to try repeatedly to master what we couldn't get easily. And we were constantly encouraged to READ, READ, READ, as if literacy were a magic key that could unlock any and all doors.

Dad worked long hours. I remember we often had to wait until past seven o'clock for his return home because we always ate dinner together. For this reason, it interests me that social scientists now point to such family routine as part of the necessary glue that binds one generation to another.

I had jobs to do inside and outside of the house and received an allowance. When I was ten, I started delivering the *Newark Star Ledger* and kept the job for four years. When I was fourteen, I began a series of summer jobs that also kept me busy. If these experiences sound typical of the way kids were raised in the forties and fifties, that should be no surprise. Mine was a wonderfully typical childhood.

My dad and mom taught me most of what I needed to know, and the community was filled with people who reinforced those lessons I got at home. And the community values seemed to be all around me. One example remains very clear in my mind. As a thirteen-year-old, I was 5'4" and weighed about 100 pounds.

Although I loved baseball, I had little power and seldom hit the ball over anyone's head.

Imagine my surprise one afternoon when I hit a ball over 200 feet and broke a school window. A tape measure home run! I was so proud of myself. However, on the way home, Mr. Herman, a neighbor of ours, called to me. "I assume you know you'll have to pay for the broken window, Saul," he said.

"Sure," I responded, "I know that."

An interesting exchange. He knew me and knew he could say what he did. There was no question in my mind that I would pay for the window, nor any question he could tell me what I had to do. There were *community* values that got reinforced.

This glimpse back into my childhood and what I learned then has stayed with me. And this was what I brought into my relationship with Eddie. Like anyone, I'm made up of a lot of different parts. Part of me is a husband, a dad, and a teacher. Part of me is also a grandfather, a Navy veteran, and a Brooklyn Dodgers fan. I have lived my whole life in New Jersey where I met my wife, Paulette, raised our children, and worked as an educator.

I started as a teacher, moved into administration as a high school principal and superintendent of schools, and served as the New Jersey Commissioner of Education from 1982-1990. After leaving that office, three years after my future friend Eddie was born, I became President of The R.E.A.D.Y. Foundation in Newark, set up to assist families with the support they needed to raise their children.

That last sentence might sound questionable to many. Why would you need an organization to assist families in raising their children? The response is that many of the families we worked with had serious problems. A single parent mom, living at or below the poverty level, headed almost all the families with whom we worked. Many of the mothers didn't have a paying job and positive male models were few and far between. Drugs were often present.

While my formative years were spent in a neighborhood that was supportive and nurturing, the Newark neighborhoods we worked in were anything but supportive and nurturing.

Anyone who has seen Newark's worst sections knows how hard it is for children to be brought up safely, surrounded as they are by things most Americans want to keep away from their children. Any day I go into Eddie's neighborhood, I am concerned about drug distribution, car-jacking, or random violence.

These are terrible enough but the day-to-day realities of life in Washington, D.C., Philadelphia, or Newark take a different type of toll on the human spirit. I'm thinking of the subtle pain that goes along with the noisy, overcrowded homes, where privacy is sometimes unknown, or the unwashed windows of homes that outnumber the soot stained leaves on the only tree on the block.

My dad's father and mother worked at their delicatessen in the North Ward section of Newark during the twenties. Their journey, like the one Eddie is beginning, had to start with steps in the right direction. My dad got the right messages as he grew up living over the store and graduated from Newark's South Side High School. His path wasn't easy and he worked hard to buy that home in West Orange.

As Eddie and I began our friendship, I found myself thinking back to some really basic parts of my own life. I had to sidestep temptations, and I'm sure I tripped over opportunities

I didn't see. I stumbled often, but my mother and father, as well as relatives and neighbors were always there to help me up and point me in the right direction. I had support and many "invisible hands" that I didn't know were working to see me raised right. My first eight years were very different from Eddie's.

As we were getting to know each other, Eddie would talk to me about his neighborhood. I remember him once saying, "See that kid on the bike? He delivers packages to drug dealers. He tells me they give him a couple of dollars every time he takes a message or package from one guy to another."

This is where he lives. Guess I'm going to have to get used to an eight or nine-year-old delivering "packages" to drug dealers. Will Eddie soon be that kid on the bike?

Eddie

Ages 8 to 11

GUNS AND VIOLENCE

"Did you ever see anyone get shot when you were a boy, Mr. Cooperman?"

The question came out of nowhere, and it startled me.

"No," I responded.

"Nobody on your block ever got shot dead? How about fights? Did you see fights with knives?"

I didn't know where the conversation was headed so I just responded to the question. I told him I lived in a place that had plenty of woods, and a friend of mine had a small "BB" gun, and I remember that he used to shoot rabbits with it. But, I told him I'd never seen or heard of a fight with a knife or a gun.

"I saw a man get shot once. We were down the block and it was summertime. We heard these weird sounds like, 'Pop! Pop! Pop!' Then James yelled and everybody ducked down behind a car. People started running and screaming. Then I saw this really dark blood on the ground coming out of this guy's head and he wasn't opening his eyes. Just then my mother came running up behind us and she grabbed my arm so hard she almost pulled it off. She dragged me all the way home and I couldn't see what else happened to the guy who got shot."

Eddie was eight when he told me about this experience – I was sixty and this was the second time we had been together. I had started the "10,000 Mentors" program in Newark, New Jersey, and naturally wanted to set an example by personally mentoring a young man. Eddie was my "man".

It may seem less than humble, but I thought I'd be a reasonably good mentor since I had taught school and helped raise three children. I also thought I knew a lot about urban America, since much of my work in the past twenty years brought me into everyday contact with city life.

As Commissioner of Education in my native New Jersey for eight years, I saw the problems of our urban centers through the eyes of teachers, parents, police and social workers. My foundation work in Newark, N.J. took me into many children's homes and my association with one of our nation's largest education reform efforts, the New American Schools, enabled me to visit and learn about the schools and neighborhoods of our major cities.

So, I felt pretty confident I could meet any challenge thrown at me by one child. Yet, I was staggered by eight-year-old Eddie's question, "You ever see anyone shot when you were a boy, Mr. Cooperman?"

Perhaps I should have been prepared for a question such as this. After all, people are killed in Eddie's neighborhood and experiences like these seem to have given him a certain fatalistic outlook on life. I learned from our initial meetings that Eddie didn't do any long term thinking because life was often short where he lived. While other children in the suburbs were talking of "the future," Eddie was thinking day to day. From his perspective, he had no reason to think otherwise.

I resolved that I had to give Eddie a sense of "future," and possibilities. I had to show him that there were opportunities open to him. But, I understood that his view of death as nothing unusual contrasted dramatically with that of my granddaughter Casey's, who is almost the same age as Eddie. After reading about death in the book *Chicken Soup for Kids*, Casey said to me, "That's not something I really have to think about now."

Casey sees a future. Eddie is not so sure. Death is around him; he knows it can happen on his block or in front of his house. He sees "Rest in Peace" murals painted on the sides of buildings to note the death (often violent) of some young person in his neighborhood. He realizes that it could happen to him. Eddie understands this, and right now I have no initial responses to his belief about the closeness of death.

Where is all my "knowledge" when I need it now?

Eddie can't compare his life with life in safe suburbs. He has no basis to make a comparison. Most of us can't either. We know one or the other. If we are poor and urban, that often means being on intimate terms with chance, random violence, accidents, routine abuse, noise, traffic, sirens, ambulances and the drop by drop doses of urban reality. If we are financially stable and live in the suburbs, life is usually different. And even if suburban lives do become interrupted with drugs or random violence, it's far less likely to happen than in Eddie's neighborhood.

One day as we were walking down his block, I noticed a man in his early twenties sitting on Eddie's steps. I asked him who the man was and Eddie replied, matter of factly, "Oh, he's a drug dealer, Mr. Cooperman, he's a nice guy."

Eddie must have seen the worried look on my face and added, "It's okay, he doesn't sell drugs in front of our house, my mom won't allow it. He sells in the house across the street. It's no big deal, Mr. Cooperman."

No big deal? Great! An R.I.P. mural at the end of the block and a drug house across the street. How do I handle this? All of these things are normal to Eddie, part of the landscape.

Maybe I'm in over my head.

18

STEREOTYPES

People have lots of stereotypes about kids like Eddie. The blackness of his skin leads to a type of stereotypical thinking. Some people assume that young black men who catch headlines for crimes they commit are representative of all black men.

So they assume Eddie is supposed to be mean, tough, angry, sullen, and potentially violent. It doesn't matter that more often than not he is soft-hearted, polite, and reasonable. If I had any doubts about that myself, they were put to rest for good one day while we were driving along the streets leading out of his neighborhood on our way to New York. We came to a light and Eddie looked out at the pedestrians as they started across the street, directly in front of us.

Burly men stepped off the curb, and mothers with carriages pushed their strollers quickly and carefully, while pulling the hands of older children in tow. Then came the sight that drew Eddie's complete attention. An old man eased himself down from the curb and began to cross behind the others. I glanced out of the corner of my eye to notice Eddie watching intently as this mini drama began to unfold. From his seat as a passenger in my car, he studied what was happening with the same intensity he used when glued to the TV set.

Other pedestrians had crossed the street by the time the light was ready to turn green. Perhaps because he rarely had the chance to ride in any car, this fairly typical scene was more engrossing for Eddie than it would have been otherwise.

By the time the old man had passed in front of our car, the light turned green and the oncoming cars began to move. Like a play unfolding for which we had front row seats, the action began to move toward a climax. One car moved slowly across the intersection at the same time the old man put his thin hand up to signal his distress. The driver of the bus opposite me kept his foot on the brake as did I, in order to avoid the danger and confusion that Eddie must have sensed growing around the scene. But, within seconds, horns began to blow from the cars stuck behind us, as drivers, who couldn't see past us, blasted their impatience.

"Don't move the car," Eddie said, over the noise. I had no chance to reply.

"That man could get hurt! How come nobody's helping him to cross the street? Why isn't there anyone to help him?"

I was taken aback by his reaction. It's likely that anyone witnessing this situation would be concerned for the old man's safety, but nothing in my previous experience with Eddie prepared me for what he tried to do next.

He told me he was going to help the old man, and began to unbuckle his seat belt. I told him to wait; I knew that letting him out on that busy street was an invitation to greater disaster. Luckily, during those few seconds, the old man managed to step toward the curb where a woman reached out to help him.

As the traffic began to flow again, things returned to normal and the potential tragedy became just a memory most of us take for granted in our big cities.

But for Eddie, it was not so easily forgotten. As I pulled away from the scene and turned right onto Broad Street, he looked back repeatedly. "That guy could have been killed," he said, straining his neck.

"Somebody should always be taking care of an old guy like that. Nothings fair about an old guy having to walk alone around here, trying to be fast and all."

I couldn't help but wonder what made him so obviously concerned. Could he have seen one of his grandparents in the old man? His mom had never mentioned Eddie's grandparents, so I asked Eddie about them. He told me about his grandmother – his mom's mother; how she used to live with them. He raved about her cooking, and even though they no longer lived together, he still got to see her. "I didn't want to move away from her, but my mom said it was for the best. We don't live with her anymore, but we visit sometimes."

I asked Eddie if his grandmother walked slowly like that man on the street.

"No, she isn't that bad off. She is not steady when she walks, and my mom makes me always open doors for granny, and I also go down the stairs slowly with her. Sometimes she holds my hand, but she's not sick like some people I see. Some old people can hardly walk at all."

I got to wondering about how all this must seem to a boy for whom speed and strength were so important, so crucial, so much a part of his ideals. His heroes, Michael Jordan and Patrick Ewing, were basketball players who were graced with tremendous God-given talent. They are strong, agile, and rich, and it's for those reasons that Eddie wanted to be like them.

Yet, Eddie didn't seem to need to distance himself from the infirm. Despite his own good health and devotion to sports, he certainly didn't seem to disapprove of those for whom such a lifestyle was, at best, a thing of the past. I was encouraged as I really admired that part of his personality.

Then Eddie started to tell me about a girl in his class, the year before. "She was half-blind and wore really thick glasses and could hardly see much at all. The other girls used to walk along beside her to keep her from bumping into things and they would also pick up stuff and hand it to her."

He paused and continued. "But once a boy in another class made fun of her and Mrs. O'Neil found out and she called that boy a dope and a jerk. That's the only time anyone ever heard Mrs. O'Neil say anything bad about a kid, but we figured she was right. It wasn't the girls' fault she was half blind and slow."

And then Eddie looked at me and said, "You have kids like that in your classroom when you were a teacher?"

"Yes, yes, I did. There were always a couple of kids who might need help from friends."

"What did you do if the other kids were mean to them?" he wanted to know. Did I think Mrs. O'Neill was right in calling the boy a dope and a jerk, he wondered? I told him I thought calling one of her students a dope or a jerk was pretty unusual, but it was probably okay, given the circumstances.

"What do you think about it, Eddie?" I wanted to know.

"I think he was a jerk and stupid, too. He's just lucky that he isn't half-blind. Then he wouldn't think it was so funny."

Eddie is one great kid. I hope the meanness of his neighborhood doesn't beat the sensitivity out of him. I don't think it will.

WHY IS SHE STARING?

The color of a person's skin has been an issue throughout American history. You can read all the books ever written about the topic but it really doesn't hit you squarely in the face until you try walking down the street with a friend who is not of the same color as you.

By January of 1996, Eddie and I had walked around his neighborhood and had gone to stores nearby where almost everyone is black. Newark itself is 70 percent African American. Eddie's experience has almost exclusively been within that realm, and he's most comfortable with what he knows. This insularity keeps coming up and dramatizes Eddie's lack of association with people who don't look like him.

Whenever we're out together, there's always a chance that someone will stare at us. But I didn't want to talk about it until he brought it up. One day we went to Penn Station to see the trains come and go. We were sitting on a bench when Eddie became aware that an elderly lady was staring at us.

"Mr. Cooperman," Eddie said, "you see that lady back there looking at us. Why is she doing that?"

"Well," I began, "you've got to admit we are a strange looking pair. I'm a sixty-one-year-old, six-foot-two white male and you're an eight-year-old, not even five foot African American boy."

"I guess so," he said, "but why do all white people hate people with black skin?"

I got defensive, naturally. But I also wanted this to be a response that any eight-year-old could understand. I knew I shouldn't start lecturing.

"Do you really think all white people hate all black people?" I asked.

"Mostly," he said.

I remembered a line from a song in South Pacific that says "You've got to be taught to hate." Obviously, Eddie had some strong negative feelings toward whites. This opinion didn't just enter his head. I needed to know why he felt as he did, so I asked him why he felt that most white people hate black people.

"My friends all say so," he said.

"Do you think I hate all black people, Eddie?"

"No, you don't, but you don't count. Mostly every white person though."

I attempted to tell him there are some people who are not filled with hate, and they have goodness in their hearts. There are many white people like that and there are many black people like that. I told Eddie that I had some African American friends I trust and that I also knew some white people whom I didn't trust at all. Then I explained that I also had white friends I would trust all the time and that I'd met some black people who are not trustworthy. There are white people who hate people with black skin, but also black people who hate people with white skin. Hate is not something that belongs to one race or group of people.

"Skin color doesn't really matter as much as the person's actions, how they deal with you and your friends. That's what really counts, not how you look."

"Well," Eddie said quietly, "I guess that's true."

He didn't seem to mean what he said. For a while I didn't say anything.

Then I said, "Do you know about Martin Luther King Jr.?"

"Sure, I do. He was a great man," said Eddie.

"He worked very hard," I said, "so that black people could have every right they are entitled to."

"What you mean by that?" he said.

"Not too many years ago, black people couldn't get in some restaurants or stay in some hotels. And they were denied their right to vote."

"I don't exactly know what voting is," he said.

It was going to be hard to discuss King's mission to bring civil rights to all Americans. I tried another tactic. I told Eddie about Martin Luther King once saying that you should judge a man by the content of his character, not by the color of his skin. I tried to explain to him that that meant what type of a person you are is what counts, whether you are honest and good or mean and bad. That it doesn't make any difference what your skin color is; it's what type of person you are.

When this didn't particularly move him, I plunged on, explaining that some people will always look at a person's skin color and not like someone of a different color. But, that is very, very wrong. I said, "Eddie, I don't agree with your friends, at all. If they go on believing that all whites are bad, then they are just as wrong as some white people who hate blacks or other people because their skin isn't white."

Eddie said he understood, but I knew that this first conversation about race wasn't going to persuade him.

"What about that time we went to that ice cream place; everyone else was white and I was the only black person in the whole place. I've never seen so many white people together at once; no black people were there except me," Eddie said.

I did remember exactly what he was talking about. We had stopped at a yogurt shop as we drove through Millburn. As soon as we stepped in, I could see him tense up. He looked around and was clearly lost. Not only did he not see anything that was familiar, but he also couldn't find anyone who looked like him. He practically turned around to walk out. Fortunately, I spotted a takeout counter where I assured him we could quickly get what we wanted.

Since that day, I always try to think in advance where I take Eddie. I intentionally stay away from places that are all black or all white. West Orange, where I grew up, has a good mix of people. When we go to play basketball there or sit in a schoolyard or get a burger, there are usually both whites and blacks around. I want him to see a larger world than his block or neighborhood where everyone is African American. I want him to see that his friends are wrong.

****

There was a day toward the end of our first year together when the topic came up in a positive way. We were at a Burger King when four teenage boys came in for lunch. They were loud as only teenage boys can be and it was impossible to ignore them as they joked and laughed and teased each other throughout the next twenty minutes. It was clear that they were friends, kids who liked each other's company. What struck Eddie most was the fact that two were white and two were black. He stared at them repeatedly while we ate. I watched him casually, without saying anything. He ate in silence. After five minutes or so, he turned to me and asked if I'd noticed them.

"Sure," I said.

"You see they were friends even though they weren't all black or white?"

"Yes, I noticed that too, Eddie." I intentionally let him do the talking, hoping that he'd reach some conclusion on his own that would click with beliefs I was trying to instill.

"Man, that's something! See, in my neighborhood, no kids would do that. Black kids wouldn't be good friends with white kids. No brothers would hang out like that. One kid was joking all the time. That was really something."

"How do you think those kids got to be such good friends?" I asked.

"Don't know. They all live in the same building or go to the same school?"

"Two of them are teammates," I said. "They have varsity jackets on. That means they play football together."

Eddie paused at this and thought a while. The concept of being someone's teammate was not a big part of his life. When he played basketball, the only sport he liked, games were pick up and his partners one day might be his opponents the next. He didn't join teams at school and was still too young to have the sense of allegiance those young men showed for each other.

"Yes", he admitted. "Maybe they are on the same team at school. That might be why they like each other so much. But, just because they're teammates doesn't mean they're friends."

I agreed with Eddie and told him so. Not only were some teammates not friends, some may not even like each other. On the field is one thing; off it is another. I didn't press the point.

Eddie continued to watch the boys and it became more evident how much they enjoyed each other's company. He was seeing but wasn't believing. What he saw was counter to his experience and that of his friends. It was hard for me not to comment, but I kept my mouth shut and made a production of drinking my diet Coke.

After the four boys got up to leave, Eddie again brought up the subject of blacks and whites as friends. He asked me what I thought about how they got to be buddies.

"Perhaps because two were teammates. Maybe the other boys were athletes, too. Or, they could live near each other and they grew up together. Or perhaps they go to the same church. But, they are friends and two are black and two are white."

Eddie had to acknowledge that, but the experience was not easy for him to accept. He questioned me several times as to "why", hoping I would somehow give him an answer that made sense to him. Of course, I couldn't and he had to struggle with a challenge to his belief system.

I discussed with Eddie the necessity of people getting along with each other. I mentioned that only one out of every eight Americans was black and that he was going to have to learn to accept and work with people who don't look like him. He was astounded by the fact that blacks weren't a majority in America. From the look on his face, I'm not certain he accepted my facts as accurate. This was our first discussion of race relations. It wouldn't be the last. I knew that one talk about what I believed wasn't going to change Eddie's opinion. Eddie had been conditioned to believe a certain way and my thoughts weren't going to change him that quickly. But at least we were talking about a very difficult subject.

WHOSE AGENDA

After Eddie and I first met, we spoke about doing a few things he never had a chance to do. We were going to take short day trips around his neighborhood and a bit beyond, so he could visit a zoo or museum in New York, as well as see a pro basketball game. Even though he lived only a mile from a major train station, he had never been on a train. Newark Airport was only slightly farther away, but he had never been there.

So, out we went to the airport one Saturday in October of 1996. It was sunny and he was all excited about this in a way that adults can't seem to remember.

"I've seen plenty of airplanes in the sky, Mr. Cooperman," he said, "but I've never seen one on the ground."

I thought that the biggest thing for him would probably be to see a huge Boeing 747 about to leave for God-knows where.

"Will there be pilots?" Eddie asked.

"Sure," I replied.

"What will they look like?"

"Oh, you'll see. They're nice. They're going to look like policemen in uniforms with hats."

"Will they have guns?"

"No, Eddie. They don't have guns. They don't need to shoot. They just fly the planes."

"Will the police be there, too?"

"No," I assured. "The police don't have to be on every plane."

I got to thinking about how Eddie's expectations about airports were dictated by his environment as well as the TV news that reports crashes and bombings and disasters, without ever saying much about the routine "blahness" of air travel. He seemed apprehensive, but also seemed to be looking forward to it all.

And all went well. We parked and walked to the closest terminal. Soon Eddie would be seeing the planes. His sense of excitement grew and grew as we got closer to the main gate arrivals. Then all of a sudden, it happened. The one thing I was most likely to take for granted and completely ignore turned into the biggest part of Eddie's trip to the airport. We walked along the ground level toward the escalator which led to where the planes were parked.

"What's this?" he chimed as soon as we stepped onto the treaded platforms. His voice was brimming. His eyes were nearly popping out of his head. He was ready to take off like a rocket ship. As we got off twenty seconds later at the top of this long ride up, he naturally wanted to know if there is another escalator that could take us down.

"What?" I asked, incredulously.

"Down. Can't we go down and take the one we just came up, Mr. Cooperman?"

"Oh, sure," I said, never wanting to miss one of those teachable moments when you're supposed to throw out the lesson plan and go with the unscheduled opportunity. So, we went down. And up. And down again. And up again and again and again and again.

The first few times were okay. We didn't interfere with those busy Americans who bring so much pent-up tension to the airports in which they race around, coming and going. Then I started feeling a little self-conscious. I thought I saw a porter staring at me descending for the third consecutive time as if he knew there was something wrong with a man my age spending time this way.

Twenty minutes into this, I gave up resisting the idiocy of it all. If it were going to be a matter of the tail wagging the dog, I thought, so be it. Eddie's pleasure wasn't diminishing at all, and I just didn't have the heart to rain on his parade.

When I think back now on that escalator rides at Newark Airport, I laugh about it. There I was, a sixty-one-year-old, riding the escalator. During my years as an educator, I had met with many very bright men and women, and I took my work to heart. I wondered as I went up and down if some of the people I worked with on important issues could see me now. I laughed inwardly as I got off the down escalator and began the next ride up.

And Eddie? He was relishing his first escalator ride as only an eight-year-old can. As I tagged along behind him, up and down the rotating stairs, I suddenly realized that ours would likely become a friendship of a different sort, one in which I would have to put aside some of my own objectives in order to let him lead me now and then. We never did see a 747. Nor did we see the rental car operation or the baggage handling that I thought would be important for him to see.

Though the afternoon was a little bit crazy to me, I began to understand that it would be necessary for me to adjust and change. In fact, as I reflect now on the day, I can pinpoint the escalator as the beginning of trying to see things through his eyes, not only through my eyes. On another level, this was my first recollection of Eddie getting what he wanted rather than I accomplishing my own goals.

I will never ride another escalator without thinking about Eddie, smiling on the way up, the way down, the way up...

JUSTICE

Frequently, Eddie would ask me about my boyhood and I would tell him about my friends and what we did. One day I had just finished telling him about my worst day playing baseball.

We had lost an important game because of an unfair decision by an umpire. I was on third base and our batter had hit a line drive that hit third base and went into foul territory. The umpire said it was a foul ball, but I knew it was fair so I touched home plate and encouraged a runner on second base who wasn't sure what to do to also come home and win the ballgame for our team. Unfortunately, the umpire didn't know the rules and my protests were to no avail. (I now know how hard it is to get umpires for sixth grade playoff softball games.)

The "commissioner" of our league rotated between the school principals in our town, and my principal, Miss MacMillan, was the "commissioner" for this particular year. I had no doubt that she would right this wrong and overrule the umpire. I also knew she liked me, and I would get the benefit if there was doubt in her mind. I was very surprised when she did not agree with me. Although I knew I was in the right and this was an unfair decision, it stuck.

But in my life, unfairness was the exception, not the rule. I felt that if you fought unfairness, you could ultimately make things right, at least most of the time. But, Eddie seems to feel that many things in his life are basically unfair and they cannot be changed. He has, on one hand, a happy personality, but on the other hand, a resigned attitude that not much can be changed. And, where there is injustice, you're not going to get much by standing up to it. Eddie was a nine-year-old with a "You can't fight City Hall" mentality.

A few months later, we had the opportunity to challenge an "injustice." We were in a diner and I had ordered a turkey burger for $4.25. When the bill came, it said I had ordered a "deluxe burger" with French fries and coleslaw at a cost of $6.75. Actually, it might have slipped by me, but Eddie and I were adding up the bill as a practical exercise in math and when I looked at the $6.75 rather than the $4.25, I said to Eddie, "I didn't order the deluxe burger. I ordered the turkey burger."

"Well, you're just going to have to pay for the deluxe because they won't change that. It'll be your word against theirs."

"Well, I'm sure the waitress will know what I ordered and what she served although it's too bad that I ate everything."

"What do you mean, it's too bad you ate everything?" asked Eddie. "Well, then I could show them it was turkey and not hamburger. They could tell the difference by looking at the plate."

"Hey, maybe what we could do," laughed Eddie, "is take a big spoon and put it down your throat and get back some of the turkey burger."

"Not a bad idea, Eddie, but that really wouldn't be worth the difference between $4.25 and $6.75. "By the way, what is the difference between $ 6.75 and $4.25?" I joked.

"Oh, man. Do we have to keep doing this? I thought you were going to try to get this changed," he said, adroitly maneuvering me back to the issue I had brought up.

I mentioned to the waitress that I had the turkey burger, rather than the deluxe, and she immediately said that she was sorry for that. She had mixed it up with another order, and she made the change.

"Boy, that was easy," said Eddie. "I didn't think that she was going to change it, especially since you had eaten everything," he grinned.

"Most people are pretty good, Eddie," I said. "If you have some facts and present them in a nice way, they usually admit that they may have made a mistake; not always, but usually."

"Well, it worked this time," he said.

At least this was a start.

When we were returning to Eddie's home, we drove by a preschool center that was called the Althea Gibson preschool. I told Eddie who Althea Gibson was and that she excelled in a sport that didn't have many black players.

He seemed interested in Gibson and her achievements. The next week I gave him a book entitled *African Americans Who Were First*. It talked about famous African American's and some lesser known individuals such as Wesley Brown, who was the first African American graduate of the U.S. Naval Academy.

During the next few weeks we read about many of the people in the book, and I thought the message of studying, working hard and persistence might be getting through. We talked about how hard it was for those people to accomplish what they did. We talked about prejudice, fairness, and justice.

"Do other people have to go through all this stuff, or only black people?" he asked.

"Lots of people have problems, Eddie." I explained what "Jewish" meant and told Eddie that I was Jewish. Sometimes people hurt me a lot and I told him about the fraternity system at Lafayette College when I went there.

"Only four fraternities would accept Jewish students although there were twenty-one fraternities. My friends had a chance to get into all twenty-one. I didn't."

I told him that, twenty years later, as a member of a Lafayette College Trustee Committee, I stayed at a Pocono Mountain resort. Although we were there to solve some of the college's problems, I took some time to walk through the hotel. I liked the laid-back atmosphere of the resort and suggested to my wife, Paulette that this would be a great place to spend a week-end.

A few months later, we decided to make a reservation. When I called, I was told that all rooms were taken. I felt uncomfortable with the tone of the employee and told Paulette that I felt the employee's voice changed when I said my name was "Saul Cooperman". She said I was probably hearing things that weren't there, but said she'd call and give a fictitious "non-Jewish" name. When Paulette called five minutes later as "Mrs. Allen Johnson", they asked her, "What type of room would you like?"

I explained to Eddie that the name "Saul Cooperman" got a rejection, while "Mrs. Allen Johnson" had her pick of rooms. Eddie understood. He understood that prejudice was often worse toward blacks, but they didn't have a monopoly on it. We talked about Asians and Italians as people who have suffered. I explained that all people have an opportunity in America, even if there is prejudice.

"You really believe that, Mr. Cooperman? You think I'll have a chance?"

"Yes I do, Eddie. In America, you've got to work to get somewhere, but in this country you can have the *opportunity*. You will have to deal with some people who won't be fair because you are black. But, there will also be good people who will judge you on what type of person you are and how well you work. And there are many of these people in our country."

"I hope you're right," he said.

Eddie was not completely persuaded that he would be given a fair chance. Many voices and experiences have taught him a contrary view. But, at least I knew he was beginning to trust me. That was important, and I hoped it would be enough for him to really listen to me. As I drove home, I was sad that a nine-year-old kid could not believe he had a chance.

EDDIE'S DREAMS

When I was nine, I wanted to play professional baseball for the Brooklyn Dodgers. At nine, Eddie wants to play professional basketball for the Chicago Bulls.

No one should discourage any nine-year-olds dreams, and I did not want to ruin Eddie's. But, I wanted to make sure jump shots did not replace reading and a cross-over dribble did not substitute for math. In Eddie's neighborhood basketball is king and schoolwork doesn't count.

All of his friends play hoops and they know the exploits of the NBA stars. On one hand, this is great. If kids play or talk sports they are staying off the street corners and away from negative influences. But if basketball becomes all consuming, as it seems to be, then I become concerned.

One day I asked Eddie, "What do you want to be when you grow up?"

"A basketball player," he replied without any hesitation.

I wasn't surprised, but asked if he was sure that's what he wanted to be. "Of course. I'm going to play in the pros when I grow up."

There was absolute certitude in his response. If this was so fixed in his mind, then I wanted to see how good he was at nine years of age. There are, after all, certain traits that can signal future possibilities. His hand and shoe size didn't seem exceptional. I had never met his dad, but Eddie's mom, Celie, said he wasn't much taller than she was. I estimated she was about five feet five inches. It didn't look like Eddie would be able to "dunk", something he always talked about.

"Do you play a lot of hoops?" I asked.

"Oh, yeah," he replied. "It's my game."

"Where do you play?"

"Up the block in the yard; I play with Anthony, Tyrone, or Keith."

"What position do you play?" I asked.

"Oh, everything," was his response. "Forward?" I asked.

"Yes"

"Guard?"

"Yes."

"Center?"

"Not too much of that."

"And how well do you dribble?"

"Oh, I'm fast. I can go full court now. But mostly we just stick to half court."

"I see," I said.

And within one week, I did see. But what I saw didn't fill me with confidence for Eddie's pro hopes. He could dribble. There was obviously a real desire in his eyes when he played. He was focused on the activity he loved in a way that I would never see in math or spelling lessons that would have us struggling together later that winter.

I would even go so far as to say that Eddie had a certain amount of style. He wasn't seamless; very few of us are at so young an age. But he did move fluently and could throw fakes with his shoulders in clear imitation of Michael Jordan or the others he watched on TV.

But there were many other giveaways that convinced me he was not extremely talented. The ball didn't go into the basket often and Eddie wasn't particularly fast for someone his age.

So, in my true educator fashion, I started where he was. I didn't feel compelled in our first exchanges to try to talk with him about realistic long-range goals that might be more attainable than a pro basketball career for someone who might top out at five feet nine inches tall. And I never bothered drawing his attention to the fact that he seemed to be carrying a few extra pounds that gave him a bulkiness which slowed him down.

I counted on having lots of opportunities to counsel Eddie on which dreams to pursue and which dreams to abandon. But, I had to start with his dream, basketball. And, as Eddie constantly pointed out to me, Mugsey Bogues is only five feet three inches and plays in the pros. I'd say the odds of Eddie becoming the next Mugsey were about one million to one! I'm sure Mugsey displayed glimpses of stardom to people who knew something about basketball when he was young. To my coaching eye – I had coached seventh and eighth grade basketball in North Plainfield, New Jersey – Eddie had little to indicate that his dream might come true. But for now, I wasn't going to tell him what I thought.

So, a quiet tug of war began. Reading versus rebounding; division versus dribbling. Since all of Eddie's friends were basketball fans and players and no one in his household was a high school graduate, the odds were not in my favor.

And, Mugsey made it, didn't he?

THE NEW JERSEY NETS

When I first met Eddie, he had never been to a pro basketball game. This topic, of course, was his passion, and, for our first few meetings he would usually begin our conversation with, "Did you see the basketball game on Monday?"

"No, Eddie, I didn't." But, this didn't deter Eddie, who would then go on to tell me who played well, who didn't, what the score was at half-time, and who were the leading scorers on each team.

I asked him if he watched the whole game, and he usually responded, "Of course." These games wouldn't end until about 10:30 at night if they were home games of the NETS or Knicks, or much later if they were playing away games in the mid or far-west.

"Sometimes I can't make it all the way through when they're playing Portland or Seattle," Eddie said.

I had mentioned the late hours to his mom on more than one occasion, but she saw no problem with Eddie staying up until midnight or later when school was in session. I made no headway in this area.

"Eddie, don't you ever get tired with all this basketball stuff?" I once asked foolishly.

"Oh, no, Mr. Cooperman; I could never get tired of basketball. It's what I like to do the best, and I watch to see the moves the players make so that I can try to do that myself."

Later that year, on a Friday night, I took Eddie to his first pro basketball game, the NETS vs. the Philadelphia 76er's. He was really wired. As we left the New Jersey Turnpike and got in line to pay our toll, Eddie was worried.

"Do we have any other tolls to pay? Will we get there on time? Will we miss the start?"

"Eddie," I reassured him, "we're only five minutes from the arena, and the game doesn't start for an hour. We have plenty of time."

After we parked and entered the arena, Eddie again became agitated.

"How are we going to find our seats in this place? How do you know where to go? I'm afraid we're going to get lost."

Only when we finally found our seats in the nearly deserted arena did Eddie start to relax. But, only for a minute. He noticed some NETS players on the court practicing their shots and his attention shifted to them.

"Would you try to get me some autographs, Mr. Cooperman? I'm kind of shy and don't want to ask the players, but maybe you could do it for me." He certainly wasn't shy with me anymore!

I knew this was really important for him, and although it didn't please me at all to be standing on a basketball court, hoping that some twenty-five-year-old multi-millionaire would sign an autograph, there I was, paper and pen in hand, with Eddie beside me.

Jason Williams, the center for the NETS, was the first one to stop by. Williams is a wise-cracking, sincere young man who is very much interested in the community and the children who live in urban America. (Unfortunately, a few years later, he accidently shot a man in his home, after a night of drinking.)

"You want my autograph, kid?" said Williams.

"Uh, huh," said Eddie.

Williams then asked, "Where do you go to school?"

Eddie responded, "George Washington Carver."

"Oh, I know that school. It's in Newark, isn't it?"

"Uh, huh," said Eddie.

"Do you study hard and are you a good student?" asked Williams.

"Not always," said Eddie, honestly.

"I'll give you my autograph, but I want you to promise that you'll work harder in school because that's really important," said Williams.

"Okay, I promise," said Eddie.

He looked at his autograph. It said "To Eddie, best of luck, Jason Williams."

"Would you please keep it until we get home, Mr. Cooperman?" asked Eddie. "I could lose it and I don't want to do that."

Shortly thereafter, Kerry Kittles, Kendall Gill and Michael Cage stopped by and gave Eddie their autographs. He was in "Seventh Heaven".

"Wait until Keith and Tyrone see these tomorrow. They won't believe it," Eddie whispered.

He was so happy with his autographs; I thought he wouldn't be able to sit through the game.

He was excited, cheering, pointing out where someone should have shot when they didn't, or when they should have passed when they shot. During this time, he consumed a hotdog, a coke, and a rather large pretzel.

At half-time, there was going to be a promotion; four children would be given large sneakers and would have to wear a baggy outfit. All "suited up", they had to dribble a ball the length of the court and attempt to make a lay-up. Every child would be given a prize and the winner would receive $100 and a special prize.

A NETS representative asked Eddie if he would like to be one of the participants. "You will be on the same court as the NETS," she said, "and you look like you can play basketball."

All the people around us were encouraging Eddie to do it, but he looked at me and said, with fear and apprehension in his eyes, "I don't want to do it, Mr. Cooperman. I'm embarrassed to go out there."

I told him that the other kids were going to be a little afraid, too, and he was probably going to be as good a basketball player as anyone else and had a good chance to make the shot.

"Besides," I said, "everyone will cheer for you anyway. They won't be mean if you fall in the big shoes."

"Well, maybe they won't, but maybe they will. Sometimes they boo the players when they don't do things right and I'm just afraid to go out there."

"Then that's your decision. I know I would probably be nervous if they said they were going to take four old men and put big shoes on them and floppy suits and ask us to go out there. I understand how you feel," I said.

I told the representative that Eddie didn't want to do it, and a very assertive young girl sitting a few seats in front of us said that she would like to do it. She was chosen and during the halftime won a pair of sneakers, a basketball, and a NETS hat.

On the way home, Eddie asked me if I was upset that he didn't participate.

"I could have shot better than that kid and might have had the chance to win the $100, but I didn't want to go out there. I was afraid that I would fall down or do something stupid. You understand?" he asked.

"I sure do, Eddie. There are lots of times in life people want us to do things, but we just don't feel right about doing them. And when you feel that way, you just shouldn't do it. There'll be plenty of opportunities in your life to compete for a basketball or $100. You had a good time at the game though, didn't you?" I said, trying to change the subject.

"Oh, I sure did. It was fun to see Jason Williams get all those rebounds. He seemed so nice when he talked with us, but he sure is tough on the court," Eddie said.

I was happy the conversation was now turning to basketball rather than his feeling that I might have been disappointed that he didn't participate.

Eddie remembered the autographs and asked for them. I took them out of my pocket and handed them to him.

"I really like these autographs. Say, Mr. Cooperman, did you ever collect autographs when you were a kid?"

"Yes, I did. I collected the autographs of baseball players."

"Did you go to the game and then ask the players before the game started?" he asked.

I told Eddie that when I went to games with my dad, we didn't get too close to the field. I didn't have the opportunity to ask as we did at the NETS game. But I told him of my method to get autographs. I used to write to players and tell them that I really liked the way they played and asked if they could sign a postcard, which I had enclosed with my letter to them. The postcard was addressed to my house.

"Did everyone sign them?" Eddie asked.

"Just about. At that time, no one charged for autographs and almost all ballplayers signed my postcards. In fact, sometimes a player must have been seated next to other players and I would get four or five signatures on a post card."

I told Eddie I could just see Jackie Robinson, to whom I wrote, sitting next to Pee Wee Reese, Duke Snider, and Carl Furillo and perhaps saying, "Hey, you guys, a kid just wrote me and asked me to sign this postcard. Will you sign it for him also?"

I liked to think that's the way it happened since Jackie Robinson was my favorite ballplayer. He not only signed my postcard, but got me the autographs of the other players as well. I told him that I was a Brooklyn Dodger fan and had many of the autographs of the Dodgers from about 1947-1950.

"Well, who were the stars of that team? Who did you like best?" asked Eddie.

"Oh, besides Robinson, I liked Duke Snider and Pee Wee Reese."

"Pee Wee?" he laughed. "Was that really the guy's name?"

"No, Eddie. That was just his nickname."

"I guess he had the name 'Pee Wee' because he was small. Is that right?"

"A lot of people thought so, but that really wasn't the reason. He got his nickname because he was really a good marble player when he was a kid and one of his favorite marbles was called a Pee Wee. That's how he got his name."

"Oh, yeah. Now you're just kidding me again. I don't believe that. He was probably small, wasn't he?" Eddie reiterated.

"I know it does sound kind of funny, but he actually wrote a letter to me because I wrote to him and asked how he got the name Pee Wee. And his letter said what I just told you."

"You're really telling me the truth, aren't you?" Eddie asked.

"Of course I am. And the next time you're at my house, I'll show you the letter from Pee Wee Reese."

"What was his real name?" Eddie asked.

"Harold," I remarked.

"I like 'Pee Wee' better," Eddie said. "Could we see the Dodgers play sometime?"

"We could, but I'm actually not too interested in seeing them play," I said.

"But I thought that was your team when you were a kid. You just don't like them anymore, right?" Eddie said.

"Well, that's right, but not just because I'm grown up. You see, the team moved from Brooklyn, which is very close to

Newark, to Los Angeles, which is across the United States. When the team moved, I was really upset and didn't like the owner of the team for doing that. So, after a few years when Reese, Snider, Robinson and other players I liked got too old to play, I stopped being a Dodger fan."

"Boy, that's really too bad," Eddie said.

He seemed genuinely moved by my disappointment in the Dodgers moving to Los Angeles. Then he continued in a way that really surprised me.

"I never like it when I see people getting let down like that. You must have been mad when the Dodgers went away."

"Yes, I was."

"Almost like the one kid who tripped over his feet and lost the ball in that half-time contest. You know, the one who didn't even get to make a lay-up."

I paused for a second to think about the connection. Personally, I didn't see how that one really fit with the other. Sure I was "bummed out" when the Dodgers left, but it wasn't like I had tried to do something and tripped in front of the Meadowlands Arena full of people. Still, I wasn't sure that I wanted to disagree with Eddie. The connection was disappointment, so I just kept listening.

"I really felt awful for that one kid tonight – not the one who made the lay-up, the one who tripped. He just wanted to get down there and try to make his shot. But that didn't happen and I thought the kid was going to get booed." He went on to say, "That's what hurts when someone wants to do something and can't, and I don't want to get let down again like that kid was."

I pondered the quick transition from the young child's disappointment, dribbling the ball with oversized shoes, to Eddie getting let down "again."

"So, when did you get let down?" I asked rather directly.

"Well, my father says he really cares about me but he really doesn't. So, he lets me down. But I'm not going to give him any chance to let me down again. If he comes, I'm not going to say anything to him," said Eddie angrily.

I finally connected the dots; a kid's disappointment at making a lay-up, my disappointment at the Dodgers going to Los Angeles, and Eddie's disappointment with his father. This hurt doesn't lie far beneath the surface.

We were both tired as we got to Eddie's house around 11:00 PM. "Thanks for taking me to the game, Mr. Cooperman. I really enjoyed it."

"No problem, Champ. I'm glad you had a good time," I said.

On the way home, I thought about a young boy and his reluctance to go out on the basketball court. I also thought about his disappointment with his dad and the hurt it was causing him. I'm not his dad. I can't be, but he doesn't have any males to look up to. I wonder how I can fill the void. I know I give him more of my time than most mentors, but he needs even more. If he had a phone, then I could call him during the week. So many "if's".

It was a great game, but I'm not feeling too good right now.

EDDIE'S ROOM

I'll never forget the first time I saw Eddie's room. I had visited his house before; I would come to the door briefly to say "hi" then "bye" to his mom or aunt. I had also been invited, quite naturally, to idle time in his living room, which is the first room you enter as you step through the front door.

There are stairs in the middle of the house that lead to the basement floor. The rooms in the basement are for Eddie, his mom and his stepbrother, Duane. When you descend from the living room toward them, the stairwell seems cramped for someone my size. I have to stoop slightly so I won't bump my head. The lighting is bad, the turns are sharp, and the stairs themselves creak a bit for want of a well-placed nail or two. There is carpeting on the stairs that's old and frayed and you have to be careful as you descend.

Three rooms lead off the basement hall. One is Celie's. The other is nearly unfurnished and contains only a TV set. Lastly, there's the 8' X 10' bedroom that Eddie shares with Duane.

Duane's bed is close to the door and away from the window. The window is small and covered with security wire on the outside. Very little light comes through. Eddie's bed is against the longer of the walls. When I saw Eddie's room for the first time, it was littered with an array of clothes, games, and the usual mess that boys are famous for creating.

Above his bed, Eddie had put up a complete wall-to-wall display of pictures and posters, all of them basketball related. Michael Jordan was flying through the air like a bird. Scottie Pippen was driving to the basket. There was Kerry Kittles popping a twenty footer, and Patrick Ewing shooting his trademark fall-away jump shot. These were the images that Eddie had chosen to idolize. And the collage that he created by tacking the pictures side by side jumped at the eye with the urgency of Picasso's *Guernica*. The slices of war or struggle in the combat of athletic competition were unrelieved for the entire ten feet.

It was exhausting to stand beneath the single light bulb that illuminated the room and to look over the colorful and poignant panorama of Eddie's gods. He had fashioned a sort of stained glass window into which he can dream himself to sleep night after night, surrounded by men whose talent, aggression, speed, and muscle have made them Olympian divinities (millionaires) for thousands of kids like Eddie.

In his room there was a conspicuous absence of other things so often associated with boyhood. There was no collection of anything – stamps, coins, cards, or hats. There were no books. There was no desk to read and study. There was no lamp, table, chair, or carpet. No closet space. No file folder or cabinet. No paper, pads, pens, pencils, or phone. There was certainly none of the technology that fills the rooms of kids who have a computer, printer or stereo system.

Eddie's room had two finger-size goldfish that swam around in a small tank with a bubbling filter, and the blue fluorescent light made the water seem "Hollywoodish." The fish were named "Big E" and "Duane", named for Eddie and his brother. They could swim from one end of the tank to the other in about two seconds. The fish tank limited the world of the fish as much as Eddie's room seemed to limit his world.

TO BOAT OR NOT TO BOAT

Eddie told me he always wanted to row a boat on a lake. For a nine-year-old, there is so much he wants to do, so many experiences he wants to have. He wanted to do this "more than anything".

When I was a kid, I remember rowing a boat in Verona Park, which isn't far from Eddie's home in Newark. One day in the summer, we drove to Verona Park and, after looking at some beautiful flowers and playing catch, we walked by the boathouse.

I said to him, "Eddie, I don't know if they still have boats here, but let me find out. If they do, we'll rent a boat. Would you like that?"

"I sure would. That would be great. You know I want to go on a boat." They didn't have rowboats anymore, but they had paddleboats where you sit and push your feet back and forth to make the boat go forward. We found that they only had three boats in operation and they were all out on the lake. When I asked the proprietor how long the boats would be out, he looked at his watch and said, "Well, they just went out about twenty minutes ago and they won't be back for another forty minutes. We rent them by the hour."

I asked him if there was anyone signed up before us and he said that there were six groups ahead of us.

I told this to Eddie and said, "The boats out there won't be back for forty minutes and there are six more groups of people who are waiting to rent the boats. How long a wait do you think we would have before we could have a boat?"

"I don't think too long. I think we should wait," said Eddie.

I knew on one hand that he wanted to take a boat ride, and that obviously was reflected in his remark. But on the other hand, I knew that he didn't want to do the math to answer the question. I persisted.

"Eddie, let's look at it this way. You tell me how long we have to wait and then we'll decide whether it's worthwhile to wait."

He struggled a bit and then said, "About an hour."

"It's not about an hour. I think you are guessing again. You've got to let me know exactly how long we have to wait. Try to figure it out. You have three boats out there now and they'll be coming back in forty minutes. Then each boat is going to go out again for another hour. When they all come back, there are three more groups of people who are going to take the boats out for another hour. That's all the help I'm going to give you. Can you figure that one out?" I asked.

"I need a pencil and paper," he said.

"Okay," I said. We walked to a place where they sold hot dogs and soft drinks and borrowed a pencil and a small piece of paper. Eddie struggled for a while but was not able to solve the problem. I then explained to him what was involved and step by step we worked through the problem. When he found out that it would be two hours and forty minutes before we got to use the boat, he said, "Oh, we can't wait that long because we told my mom that we'd be back by six o'clock. We wouldn't even get the boat until after six o'clock."

"That's right. But if we hung around here, we would be waiting and waiting and then after a while you would realize that we weren't going to get the boat and we would have wasted the time just sitting on our rear ends. That's why math is important," I said.

"Yeah, when you look at it that way, I guess it does make some sense. But I really wanted to go on a boat ride."

Now that we were into the second year of our friendship, he's getting used to me and knows that whenever time, money, or distance is involved I'll probably turn it into a practical math problem. He doesn't seem to mind, but his batting average for solving these problems isn't good.

We made reservations for the next week, and Eddie and I took our boat ride. He had a great time paddling furiously around the lake. We "attacked" make believe "pirates" on an island, paddled to a water fountain and got sprayed, and tried, unsuccessfully, to sneak up and scare some ducks. We went from one end of the lake and back again and raced to overtake another boat that became our "competition."

When the hour was over, I was thankful to reach shore. Although I work out every day, there were muscles that quite obviously hadn't been used. Eddie was thrilled with the boat and asked, "When can we do this again?"

"Maybe next year, Eddie," I wheezed as I pushed my aching legs to move.

Maybe I've got to do more than the treadmill and Nordic Trac.

ELIZA AND EDDIE

I remember Professor Henry Higgins saying, when he first saw Eliza Doolittle, that it wasn't her wretched dress and dirty face, it was her "oohs" and "oows" that kept her in her place. Higgins, of course, was referring to Eliza's language, her inability to speak properly and be understood by others. He figured that if he could change her speech, her grammar, and her vocabulary, he could pass her off as an upper- class woman.

I wasn't interested in superficial changes that would "pass off" Eddie as something he was not, but I was concerned about his language. Eddie used the word "be" as a substitute for other verbs, such as "He be real good, Mr. Cooperman," or, "Where he be at?" This was just one of Eddie's poor language patterns and although I usually understood what he was saying, I knew it would not be helpful to him in the long run to fracture the language as he was doing.

I talked with Eddie's favorite teacher about his reading ability and, while doing so, brought up his language usage. She said, "Maybe we compromise too much, but these patterns are reinforced with friends and family. It's most difficult to change how the kids speak. And besides, these children need so much work in the basics; there isn't enough time to even consider working on their speech."

I mulled this over for quite some time and thought perhaps I would work on one thing and just keep at it until, at least in my presence, Eddie would change. Then, when that occurred, move on to another area. But there were so many things to do. There were his attitudes, his belief that he would never leave his neighborhood; the belief that he might not live to age seventeen; his habits of watching TV until midnight on a regular basis; doing homework "sometimes;" feeling that all whites hate blacks, etc.

I thought hard about my responsibilities as a mentor. If I am to mentor Eddie, shouldn't I have an idea of what it is that I feel is important and what I want to communicate to him and what I want to model? If I don't challenge him about the way he speaks, am I not condoning and accepting his language as satisfactory?

I talked this over with Paulette and decided that working on his language would be a full time effort, and would drive a wedge between Eddie, his family, friends and me. Other things were more important. Part of me felt like I was making a bad deal with myself, to lower my goals and expectations and not give Eddie all the chances he deserves to move ahead in our competitive society. I felt a little hollow inside that I was letting him down by not being stronger with him.

I remembered the innumerable times with my own children when they would become upset with me and say, "But everyone does it," or, "You're really out of it, Dad. Your approach went out in the fifties." But I believed then, as I believe now, that the values you believe in and the character you are trying to build in children are among the most important things you can do as a parent. This requires, at times, sucking in your gut, defining and enforcing limits and saying, in effect, this is what I believe, and what I expect of you.

I was "tough" with my kids and years later they all at least understood my approach. Was I not being "tough" with Eddie by allowing him to speak in urban America as Eliza spoke in urban England?

Possibly, but I have not made a habit of correcting Eddie in his use of language. Every once in a while I will correct him, letting him know that "where he go" isn't what he should say. I tell him the right way to say it and that is all. I reason that it's a situation of what is more important, and I have put values and character development at the top of the list followed by acceptable performance in English and math. Acceptable to me will be performing at grade level. I'm resigned, at present, to not correcting Eddie's speech. If the other things get done, then I may deal with his speech.

And, in this story, when I quote Eddie, I have chosen to use proper English throughout. I think it is enough to point out here that this is the way I hope Eddie will ultimately speak, but not the way he always speaks now.

BOOKS

Eddie tells me that he knows education is important because he knows that is what I want to hear. But, his actions do not follow his words. This has been an on-again off-again point of contention for us. I suspect it will continue to be an issue we're not going to frequently agree on.

Some of our earliest exchanges had me sitting in the local library with Eddie, helping him read some of his assignments while he did his homework. "Why didn't you look up the words, Eddie? There were only five of them," I asked.

"I forgot."

"Really, even when I called you yesterday to remind you?" (Celie had a phone installed about a month ago.)

"Why should I learn the word 'integrate'? I'm not using it so why should I know it?"

I was prepared for this type of remark and took out a story I had in my coat pocket. I asked Eddie to read two pages, which he did. I then asked him what the story was about and he couldn't do it because he didn't understand several key words.

"See, Eddie, this is why words are important. They allow you to *understand* what you read. If you don't know the key words, you can't know what's going on."

"Uh huh – I guess…"

****

Eddie is in the fifth grade and he makes mostly "Ds" on his report cards, with an occasional "C" thrown in. He has made one "B" in his core subjects and also and "F." He's the sort of kid who just wants to get by. And a "C" in Eddie's school might be a failing grade in a good suburban school.

One day I gave Eddie a dictionary, and he was very appreciative. He said it was great to have his own dictionary. As we saw words in a newspaper, a shopping mall, or on a menu, I gave him an assignment to look these words up and use them in a sentence. This went well for the first two weeks, and then the "game" was over. He simply "forgot" or "couldn't find the dictionary". I've tried to interest Eddie in library books. He showed some initial interest, however he never reads with any degree of understanding. We've tried vocabulary flash cards based on his reading, but that hasn't worked either. With his mother's support and Eddie's spoken interest, we began to read the Junior Great Books. These are interesting stories from a wide range of cultures and each story has a real "punch" to it.

Every once in a while, he would read a story and have some understanding. But, mostly, it just wasn't important to him and his lack of effort showed it.

"Eddie, you say you know it's important to read well, but you don't make any effort to do better. Do you think something magical will happen and suddenly you'll be a good reader?"

"I know I have to do better, but it's hard for me."

"I won't accept that. You work hard on your head fakes and crossover dribble, and I see improvement. You improve because you work at it. You don't work on your vocabulary, so how can you improve your reading?"

"I want to do better. Sometimes I forget to bring my books home."

"That's a bunch of crap, Eddie. You know it, and I know it."

I was losing my cool and wouldn't get anywhere by doing so. I know he sees no value in reading. Celie tells him that she regrets dropping out of school and that Eddie must graduate from high school. But, that is so far away to Eddie that it doesn't register. How in the world do I get him to see the value of reading well?

I knew a dangerous pattern of failure was developing. Just as success breeds success and encourages kids who do well to continue to do well, there is a similar current that sweeps through the lives of children who fail. Discouraged, fatigued, impoverished, they soon establish self-defeating routines that keep them from catching up with their peers in suburban schools.

These patterns were there. Most of his friends didn't care about school so why should he? Eddie told me that older kids put down anyone who does well, saying they are 'acting white.' He doesn't see anyone who reads for pleasure.

I've never been so frustrated.

ABSENT

I talked to Eddie about his attendance after he completed the fifth grade.

"Eddie, you must do better in school attendance. You were absent nineteen times and tardy ten times. You can't learn if you're not in school."

"I can't help it, Mr. Cooperman, sometimes my throat or stomach hurts, and my mom thinks its best I stay home and rest."

"Do you mind if I talk to your mom about this?"

"No, go ahead. Besides, the school doesn't have the truant officer bring you in until you are absent twenty days."

Damn! He may have been only ten, but he understood how the system worked, and he knew he could avoid school for nineteen days without any repercussions.

I talked with Celie and she backed up Eddie's story. "He says his throat hurts, his ears hurt, or his stomach hurts. I don't want to send him if he's sick."

"Perhaps you could take him to the clinic when he complains of an ear problem or throat problem. A doctor can usually see if something is wrong with the ears or throat. The stomach is a lot harder to determine without tests." I was becoming upset, and tried once more; "A truant officer comes once a kid is absent twenty days, and Eddie was absent nineteen. It seems suspicious to me. What do you think?"

"I guess you think he may be lying, don't you?"

"Yes – I think he is. He wouldn't be the first kid to use sickness as a way to stay home."

"I believe Eddie. I just do."

Celie is great and she wants Eddie to do better, but won't confront his absenteeism or failure to do his homework. She does care, but there are so many other things to worry about that she doesn't expend the energy necessary to get Eddie to make education a high priority.

I'll continue to get verbal support for my efforts, but not much help from Celie on a day to day basis with attendance, homework, and substituting some books for the TV.

How can this work? Maybe I should just bag it and work with people who value my opinions. I'm discouraged.

****

Eddie thinks I'm smart and has said things like "You ought to be on 'Jeopardy', Mr. Cooperman. You'd clean up."

I know he thinks I can answer every question he asks, and on several occasions he has told me how impressed he is with my "knowledge". I tell Eddie I don't know as much as he thinks I know and often I take papers home because I have to work on them. I've shown Eddie my "homework" and have told him all the things I don't know and have to figure out. I explain to him that like school kids, I often do my "homework" after dinner.

"See, Eddie, adults do homework, too. If I do mine poorly, I don't get a 'D.' I might not get a raise, or if I do a very bad job, I might get fired."

We've been to my office several times, and Eddie has seen me working at my desk while he does his homework at a table next to me. Whenever we have been at my office, I always appear to be stumped by a word and ask Eddie to look it up for me.

Devious!

On my part, it will be a delicate balancing act, not just trying to model but also to prod. Yet, in the end, Eddie must see what I'm selling as purposeful. I will try to "hook him" one way or another, but it will take his responsiveness as well as my initiative.

Maybe I can get some successful African Americans to tell Eddie how important academics were in their lives. Maybe it would have impact from someone other than his teachers, his mom, or me.

ANDRE AGASSI – IMAGE IS EVERYTHING

A few years ago, Andre Agassi, the tennis player, was in an advertisement whose tag line was "Image is Everything". Looking good was to be valued more than substance.

Eddie had never seen Agassi's ad, but his back to school plan in 1997 seemed to be following in the tennis star's footsteps. He had new sneakers. He had two pairs of stylish baggy pants and several new Tommy Hilfiger shirts. These clothes, in addition to others he had, were certainly going to make him a well-dressed young man. On one hand, I felt good for him because he was eager to wear these new clothes. Yet, on the other hand, as I would often look about the apartment, with a minimum of furniture and conveniences, I felt bad because so many of the precious dollars were being spent on clothes.

Most kids get some new clothes when they go back to school. Yet, Eddie always seemed to have plenty of clothes. It would be weeks before I would see the same shirt or pair of pants being worn. The outward image was important to Eddie.

"Eddie, you look good," I said to him on a beautiful October afternoon. "I like your shirt and pants. The only thing missing are your books. Where are they?"

"Most of the time, we can't bring the books home because we have to share them with another kid in the class," he said.

I told him I found that hard to believe. I knew that his school had received additional monies from the state and from what I'd read in the paper, the superintendent said all the kids had books. Eddie didn't agree with this and told me he only had a math and science book. The other books had to be shared and he couldn't bring them home.

I said to Eddie that I thought I'd see his principal if he didn't mind. He didn't. The principal told me all the students had their own books since the first day of school. When I confronted Eddie, he said they "just got books a few days ago."

"Eddie, I'm really ticked off. You didn't bring your books home and then made up a story. What a bunch of garbage! You expect me to tell the truth, and I expect the same from you."

He gave me a contrite look and said he wouldn't lie to me "ever again". I had made my point and decided to change the subject somewhat.

I remembered that we had attended a Christmas party the year before and Eddie was given a New Jersey NETS gym bag. I suggested that the gym bag would be a way to carry his books home. "But, the NETS stink," he said. Then realizing he got it because I had taken him to the party, he diplomatically added, "but it's a good bag."

Putting on my most optimistic face, I said that the NETS would be a good team in a year or two, and he would have the gym bag of a winner. A mistake – Eddie knew basketball and he told me why the NETS would not be winners.

Just when I thought this discussion was going nowhere, he said, "I guess I could use it to carry my books, even if some kids will tease me."

****

A few weeks later, I arrived at Eddie's home before he got there and I was pleased to see him coming down the block, his NETS gym bag firmly in his right hand. "I see you have your NETS bag. Do you have any books in it?" I asked.

"Of course, I do. I bring them home every night, just like I said I would."

It was a start and it looked like he was working on something of substance. I wasn't quite ready to discuss my feelings of image and substance with Eddie. But, I just wondered about Andre Agassi making advertisements stressing image is everything when I knew how hard he had worked to get himself in superb shape and lift himself from a ranking of about 120 in the world to being consistently in the top five. He did that because of substance. 'Image' was important to Eddie, as it was to many of his friends, and indeed, probably to a lot of American pre-teens. But the NETS bag represented a small triumph for 'substance'.

MY FEARS

When my own son and daughters were growing up, I'd look critically at toys to consider whether there might be some kind of hazard. Parents are forever being warned about such dangers. When each of my children got to be ten, Paulette and I transferred our concerns toward bike safety, falling from trees, and who their playmates were.

After knowing Eddie a while, I began to worry about him too. From time to time, I'd think about him. He's ten now and no longer the little boy who held my hand when he was eight. Maybe I'd see a photo of some kid who looks like him. Or maybe I'd hear a voice that reminds me of him. Then I'd start wondering how he is, what he's doing, if he's smiling, if something is wrong, or can I help him.

If you're like I am, you don't need to be reminded how things can get bad very quickly. The earthquake coverage or last night's news of an auto accident is enough to sharpen your awareness of how fragile human happiness can be. The sadness of so much misfortune is spotlighted by headlines so often that some people think life is all chance.

I don't and I never will.

But, I do know sometimes something can rush into our lives with an apparent haphazardness. It creates havoc. In an instant, it can turn health to sickness, drain fortunes, flood farmland, or topple mountains.

When my imagination gets going with things that face Eddie, it can get pretty nightmarish. If I hear a radio announcement about some incident in Newark, a drive-by shooting, robbery, or drug bust, I immediately become anxious for his welfare.

I might turn off the radio or divert my attention to something else in the hope of not letting some paranoia take control. But then I'll find myself musing a few minutes later on what could have occurred.

Could Eddie be the innocent child who was wounded in the crossfire? Could he have been hurt playing with his friends in an abandoned house?

My worse fear, of course, is that Eddie might be killed accidentally. I'm sure that his mom, Celie, is never going to let guns become part of Eddie's life.

Still...

Like anyone else who frets over loved ones, I will occasionally give in to fear and see some bad scenarios. I'll put a tragic ending on a play-in-progress and wonder how heartbroken I'll be if Scene Three ends with me very upset because I, an older man, outlived a boy who never had a chance to get off the ground.

It's a short distance between my home and Eddie's, probably about twenty-five miles. I'm sure, too, that there are many situations where it's only twenty-five miles between poverty and upper middle class suburbia.

Unbelievable. If Eddie lived where I lived and had all the chances that kids have in Bernardsville, New Jersey, I honestly believe things would be different. But he lives in Newark and I live in Bernardsville and they are worlds apart.

I may be somewhat foolish, but as I drive from my home to Eddie's and see the clean lawns deteriorate into streets littered with paper products and empty containers, I still think Eddie has a chance.

I've changed somewhat in the way I hope and worry. In some ways, I am more confident about Eddie's future because I know him better and see an innate goodness in him. He is a good person; I'm confident of that, and he has a loving mother who will protect and provide for him. But, I still worry the neighborhood will swallow him.

TELLING THE TRUTH

"It's time for lunch. Put away the basketball," Paulette called again.

The first time we had Eddie to our house, Paulette had taken some care to prepare what he liked most: fried chicken, macaroni and cheese, and orange juice. Eddie and I had been playing basketball in the driveway.

We came into the house, washed up, and sat down to eat.

Eddie tore into the food. "This is the best chicken and macaroni and cheese. You sure are a good cook, Mrs. Cooperman."

After lunch, we were playing a board game at the kitchen table, and Eddie asked where the bathroom was.

"Just go up those steps, Eddie, and then turn left. You'll see it," I said.

Off he went, up the steps and into the bathroom. A few minutes later, he came down and we resumed our game.

About fifteen minutes later, I said to Eddie, "Now it's time for me to go to the bathroom. Think about your next move."

As I walked across the kitchen and up the steps, I continued on to the end of the hall and into our bedroom where there is another bathroom.

When I came back, Eddie said, "You didn't tell the truth. You didn't go to the bathroom, Mr. Cooperman." He was challenging me and looked hurt.

From the first day we met, I had emphasized telling the truth. At that time, I told Eddie that he could depend on me for two things. I said that I would always tell him the truth and I would always keep my promises. I had held to that, but now I was being challenged, and didn't know why.

"You didn't tell me the truth. You didn't go to the bathroom," he said again.

"But I did go to the bathroom, Eddie. I went up the stairs and into our bedroom. There's a bathroom next to our bedroom and that's where I went," I said.

"You mean you have two bathrooms?"

How very different our lives are.

PROTECTION

Eddie wanted to know how I protected Paulette when I was away on business trips. He thought I was lax by not having a gun in the house and teaching her how to use it. He also thought the woods behind our home were dangerous. "Wild animals might live there – they could hurt her if she went outside."

While he was comfortable in his neighborhood of drug dealers, car thieves and constant violence, he was afraid of woods populated by deer, squirrels, and chipmunks. And he worried about Paulette's safety.

I live only twenty-five miles from Eddie, but, once again, I am reminded that our worlds are much farther apart.

THOREAU

I wanted Eddie to "hear" the silence of the woods and see all that was going on amidst the apparent quiet. I wanted to open this window and show him the beauty of nature. If I could just get him started, curiosity and interest would take over. Or would it?

I thought back to when I was working in Trenton, New Jersey. I had recommended that a colleague of mine, who was from St. Louis, Missouri, get an apartment in nearby Lawrenceville. She took my advice, but after three months told me she was going to move to Trenton. She said she couldn't stand the quiet. "The only thing I hear at night is the sound of crickets." I remembered the Salem cigarette ad, "You can take her out of the city, but you can't take the city out of her."

I was coming to realize that my young friend was not one to listen to crickets either. I still believed my efforts in opening nature's windows would be helpful to him, not out of a sense of ego, but the feeling that most kids like to see squirrels play, chipmunks run about, and ants at work. But, it was also clear that destiny had dealt Eddie some cards that would be difficult to overcome. The city was becoming part of him.

Maybe a walk in the woods with Eddie wasn't such a good idea at this time. When I stay within Eddie's experiences, everything is okay. But, when I move too far from his world, he can become nervous and upset. Maybe the key is moving the boundaries of what he knows back somewhat, but not too far. Maybe a visit to a local arboretum will work?

MOTIVATION AND VALUES

Eddie is ten and still crazed about basketball; not baseball, football, soccer, or tennis, only basketball. He still has the same wild pipe dream shared by many of his friends; of making it to the pros. He's even said that when he does become a rich superstar, he won't forget me. "I'll give you front row seats to all my home games!"

Within this fantasy, some reality and goals have set in. He wrote a letter to me to thank me for a birthday present and said in it, "I'd like to live in a house like yours and be married to someone nice like Mrs. Cooperman." Just a little guy's thoughts but something I could work with, and ideas flooded my head.

Soon after that comment, he was admiring my car and asked about the cost. I told him the price was approximately $20,000. I reminded him of his comments about our house and told him that you could buy a house with only a fraction of the total cost. On we went to discuss how much the down payment was and how much I have to pay each month for the house. A few weeks later, he was back on the same subject, wanting to know how much down payment one would have to make for a car, and how much the monthly payment would be.

I said to Eddie that we would find out from a new car dealer since we were headed up Springfield Ave. and there were plenty of new car dealers in Summit and South Orange. I stopped at the first dealer I saw, a Ford dealership, and we walked in. I introduced myself and Eddie and the salesman understood after a few brief comments that this was an educational, not a buying situation. Since it was four in the afternoon and we were the only people in the showroom, he was most gracious with his time. Slowly Eddie became more interested.

"Which one do you like, Eddie?" the salesman asked.

"The one over there, the dark blue one," he said pointing to a Mercury Marquis.

"I thought you would like one of the smaller, sportier models," said the salesman.

"I like this one because it looks big and powerful. How much does it cost?" asked Eddie.

"If you bought it just as it is, it would cost $23,000."

Eddie asked me quietly how much money we would have to put "down" and how much would we have to pay each month. I did some quick figuring and said if we had $5,000 to put down payments might be about $850 for two years. The salesman smiled at my math and said, "That's a pretty good figure. Do you have $5,000 for me, and can you pay $850 a month for two years?" Eddie looked at me and I said, "That's the way it's done. But, I'd have to show that I had a good job and would make the payments each month. Otherwise, it would be foolish to give me a brand new car if I weren't a good risk to make the payment each month."

All of this was new to Eddie. His mom and aunt work hard at their jobs but don't bring home much money, and major purchases such as cars are out of the question. He's had no lessons on saving. No lessons on delayed gratification. No experiences with allowances that would enable him to start regarding money as anything more than a heap of coins. Nickels, dimes, and quarters slip through his fingers. If you have it, spend it. "Live for today" is the motto Eddie sees modeled by the adults in his life. And he adopts that attitude as a result.

****

When I retired from my job as Commissioner of Education, there was a farewell dinner held in my honor. There were 700 people in attendance and people said a lot of nice things about me, as they usually do on such occasions. But, the most moving comments were made by my thirty-year-old daughter, Suzanne. In part of Suzanne's remarks, she told how she earned money for various chores when she was little. "I remember dad made me save some of the money I earned. I wanted to spend it all! But he told me to set a goal for a big purchase; if you work hard and save some of your money, you'll be surprised how soon you will be able to buy it! And I did. I got an 'Easy Bake Oven'."

I was touched that she would remember that lesson. That's what I hope Eddie might say when he is thirty. But, Suzanne was under our roof every day and Eddie isn't. She had work to do around the house and earned her money. She remembers. He's too young to get a job and earn money. Maybe when he's older I can convince him to save for a major purchase. But, for now I'll try to make the connection between academics and earning power, especially since I don't believe he has any chance of becoming a professional ball player.

The connection between academic success and money remains elusive. Eddie understands the "lesson" of the Mercury Marquis and that a person must have a good steady job in order to drive out with a new car when only a fraction of the worth is given as a down payment. An understanding of the relationship between good grades and a good job just isn't there, yet.

I thought perhaps pegging Eddie's grades to financial reward might work. Generally, I don't believe in giving kids money for good report cards, but with Eddie I made an exception. "Get B's in English and math and I'll take you out to eat, to the movies and give you $20.00," I told Eddie. I did this for two reasons.

Most importantly, it linked education and money. I wanted him to see the relationship. And, second, because Eddie has no way at home to earn money, it might be a motivator. I'm not raising my hopes that this will jump-start Eddie academically. But, I'm willing to give it a shot.

I think when he is older and able to work during the summer, I can get him a job with one of my friends. This will keep him away from the bad elements in his neighborhood and teach him that work isn't easy. It will also put money in his pocket.

Maybe I can convince Celie to let me open an account for him at a bank and save 20 percent of what he earns for a major purchase. It just might work.

It worked for Suzanne, but Suzanne is my daughter and I kissed her when she woke up and when she went to bed. She loved my stories of Manduck (half man, half duck). And, Manduck, amongst his crazy escapades, talked about studying hard, working hard and saving. Manduck often talked Suzanne and then Debbie to sleep. I could hold these little girls and love them every day of their lives. Eddie lives twenty–five miles away and Eddie's father doesn't talk to him at night.

VEGGIE

As we were walking down the street, Eddie said to me, "You're really nice to me. When I'm older and get a good job, I'm going to do things for you. I'm going to take you out to eat and take you to places you want to see."

"I'm counting on it," I said smiling. "You know, I'm getting older, and there's going to be a time when I'm not going to take you out all the time because I'll be retired. Then, I'm going to depend on you to take me out. And when that happens, I'm going to order a lot of food so you better be prepared."

Eddie laughed and said, "That's okay. You can eat all you want, and I'll pay for it because that crazy stuff you eat doesn't cost much."

The "crazy stuff" was a diet low in fat, with plenty of fruit and vegetables. I eat this way because in 1990, I discovered that I had high blood pressure. Various tests determined that several of my main arteries were blocked to some degree, but not yet candidates for surgical treatment.

"You must begin to take some medication; you're going to have to watch your diet. Cut down on sugar, salt, and fat," my cardiologist said.

At first, I was quite upset, because I had taken good health for granted. But I shouldn't have, since my genetic inheritance was not particularly good. My dad had died at sixty-one and my mother at fifty-eight, both of heart attacks.

So, I began to watch what I ate. Converts to anything can be insufferable. And, as my knowledge grew, I became more and more aware that what I had been eating and loving was the standard American diet of meats, cheeses, and rich desserts. So now I had become an eater of tree bark, grass, and wild berries as my friends kept reminding me.

When we went to our favorite McDonald's to have a burger, Eddie noticed that I only ordered a diet Coke. In fact, on several occasions, I took out a bag that contained some raw vegetables. I asked him if he wanted any. With a face that looked as if he were reacting to poison, he said, "That's nasty stuff, Mr. Cooperman. I'm not going to eat any of that."

I persisted and asked him to try something, which he did. "It's *really* nasty. I don't understand how you can eat this stuff," he said, after eating a sugar snap bean.

One day, after we finished taking a walk, I offered Eddie a plum.

"What's that?" he said.

"A plum," I said, surprised that he had to ask.

"What does it taste like?" he inquired.

"Try one," I suggested.

"No way. I'm not eating anything like that."

＊＊＊＊＊＊＊＊＊＊＊

Later in the day, while we were sitting under a tree, Eddie mentioned that I didn't have a nickname. He said he could be called Ed or Eddie, but Saul didn't seem to have a nickname.

"I'm going to give you a nickname," he said.

"Don't you think I'm a little on in years to be given a nickname now?"

"Well, I feel kind of sorry for you, without any nickname, or even a middle name. Most people have one, you know," he said as a mischievous smile came across his face. Eddie often has an interesting sense of humor; he can gently poke fun, and obviously that was what he was doing now.

"Actually," I said, "there are people who call me 'Coop'. Anyone who has a name of Cooper or Cooperman is usually called 'Coop'." I told Eddie that three people call me "Chief", two call me "Coach", and two "Professor". I asked if he liked any of those.

"I don't like those names. You've got to have a good name."

Across the street from where we were sitting was a pizza parlor, and I said to Eddie, "What about pizza? That's your favorite food and so maybe you could call me 'Pizza'," I said.

He thought for a minute and concluded that "Pizza" was not a good name. "I don't like that, but I've got a good one," he said with great enthusiasm. "I'm going to call you 'Veggie' because you're always eating those awful vegetables. That's what I'm going to call you, 'Veggie'."

He was so elated with his nickname that I met his enthusiasm with strong agreement. I told him I was happy with the name. "So, from now on, you can call me 'Veggie'." Now we were on somewhat equal ground, both with nicknames. He was pleased and so was I.

Then he added, "But, I'll only call you 'Veggie' when we're together. Otherwise, I'll still call you Mr. Cooperman. Is that okay?"

"It's a deal," I said.

Eddie

Ages 11 to 16

THE TESTING OF EDDIE

"Mr. Cooperman, when you were younger, did you ever do drugs?" I told him I didn't, but asked him why he was questioning me. "Some older kids were drinking beer and they asked me if I wanted some. I told them 'no' and then they asked me if I wanted some pot."

"Did you?" I asked.

"No. I didn't want to do that. But they told me it wouldn't hurt me, and I'd feel really good."

"Don't they tell you about pot and other drugs in school?" I asked Eddie.

"Sure, they do, and they show us movies and the nurse comes in and tells us how bad it is for us. But I see adults and kids not much older than I am who drink and take drugs. Most of them seem just fine."

"Do you think that drugs are okay?" I asked.

"No, no," he said. "There are some drugs that are no good because they can kill you. But other drugs don't kill kids. They just seem to make them have more fun."

"It may not seem dangerous," I said, "but it can have a very bad effect on you through the years. You know sometimes you don't see your hair growing, but you know it's growing when it's time to have a haircut. And you might not see some bad things happening inside your body until something bad happens and it's time to see the doctor. Do you understand what I'm trying to say?"

"Yeah, I do, and that's what the school nurse is always saying. Well, you didn't take drugs, but did you ever smoke cigarettes?" Eddie asked.

I surprised him by saying, "Yes, I did. I used to smoke a lot when I was in the Navy. It often got pretty boring when we were at sea and I would sometimes smoke two packs of cigarettes in one day."

"But, you don't smoke now, do you?"

"No, I don't. I stopped smoking when I was twenty-five, the day my first daughter was born."

"Well, I don't smoke cigarettes, and I don't think I ever will," said Eddie emphatically.

I was wondering why he was so strong- willed about cigarettes as being harmful, but not thoroughly convinced that some drugs were harmful. When I asked him why he was so against smoking cigarettes but not as concerned about certain types of drugs, he said, "My mom said she knows people who died because they smoked cigarettes. But I've never seen people die from smoking pot."

Eddie certainly has lots of company with this line of reasoning, and I didn't see that I could convince him about that at this time. I resolved that this issue was not ended and I would return again and again to try to convince Eddie that he should not smoke anything.

As I drove home that night, I thought about such great thinkers like Reinhold Niebuhr and Martin Buber who wrote about the behavior of moral people in immoral societies. I thought about Eddie being faced with similar issues in his own private decision-making process. Why should he act in the manner that I recommended when so many people around him were choosing unhealthy lifestyles? How can we expect young people to behave well while so many of the people they see are acting in a contrary way?

And I thought of the power his mom had on him in certain areas. Even though he couldn't *see* people who smoked get sick and die, Celie said she had seen people die from cigarettes and that was sufficient for Eddie.

But the "testing" of Eddie by neighborhood forces was beginning. I know most kids will be offered liquor and some drugs before they graduate from high school. It happens in the wealthiest of suburbs as well as urban communities, but, eleven-year-olds!?

How can this kid have a fair chance when he is approached at eleven? Most kids look up to their older "friends" for guidance. Some guidance! And they are like bees buzzing around him while I'm in Bernardsville.

I had hoped that Eddie and I wouldn't have to talk about these issues for a few more years. Obviously, I was wrong. But, I felt good that he would talk to me so I could have a chance to counter the influence of the "street".

RUTGERS LIBRARY

We talked about football on and off for the hour it took to get from Eddie's house to Rutgers' home field in Piscataway. We parked in the lot and then took our two chairs and ate our sandwiches and soft drinks. Eddie was amazed by all the people waving pennants and dressed in the red color of Rutgers University.

The game really didn't test our knowledge of football as the opponents from West Virginia raced up and down the field, scoring at will. Near the end of the second quarter, the score was something like 31 – 0, and Eddie's interest was taken up more by the Rutgers "knight" riding around the perimeter of the field on a beautiful white horse, than the activities on the football field.

"Why is that guy dressed up like that? He looks silly with all that stuff on him."

I explained to Eddie that Rutgers' symbol is a scarlet knight, and that launched a discussion of the way warriors dressed in medieval times.

"I remember seeing guys dressed like that on TV," said Eddie. "Maybe they wore that then, but it seems stupid to be wearing it now."

I had to agree and thought the guy on the horse must have been pretty warm underneath all that armor on this beautiful October day.

We left after halftime and then it was my time to get in a little education. We drove around the main campus and Eddie thought he'd never seen so many young adults in one place. We walked into the library and saw students studying even though the day was beautiful.

"Why are these people studying? Don't they have anything better to do?" asked Eddie.

"Well, this is a university, and each one of these students studying wants to learn something, and the only way they're going to learn is to read." I started a small discourse on the ability of human beings to access knowledge and to be able to learn almost anything we desire, as opposed to animals who only know things by instinct and a minimal amount of teaching that is possible for some species.

Eddie had already turned me off and wanted to know why there were so many books. This was my opportunity, "Let's see if we can find a book in the library. A man by the name of Ernest Boyer writes books about education. Let's find some books by him."

"How are you going to find a book in this big place? Where are you going to begin to look?" asked Eddie.

Although I needed help with the computer, we ultimately found a book by Boyer in the stacks. Eddie was amazed that I was able to do this. "How did you find that place? What did you do to get that book?"

I launched into a very short lecture on the Dewey Decimal System and how it was relatively easy to find a book even in such a large place as the Rutgers' library. The computers made the job even easier

"Let's find another one, Mr. Cooperman. Let me try it," said Eddie.

What a breakthrough, I thought. This was the first time I could remember Eddie wanting to perform an academic task. Sure, it was still a game to him, but it was a good game. We spent another twenty minutes going up one isle and down another, with gentle hints from me until Eddie found his book.

"This isn't so hard after all," he said.

"No, it isn't," I said. "If you want to learn things, books are where you usually have to go. And now you have a pretty good idea of how to track down books in a library." (The present practice uses online library searches, but this wasn't available when Eddie and I visited the Rutgers University Library.)

"I think I can remember how to do it," said Eddie. "Thanks for showing me."

Well, well...

VOTING AND THE ENVIRONMENT

"Would you like to see how adults vote?" I inquired on the phone when Eddie and I spoke on the Sunday before Election Day in 1997.

"What?" he asked.

"Voting, Man. Tuesday is Election Day, and I'm going to vote. Would you like to go with me?"

"Where do we have to go?" he said.

"Back where I live, in Bernardsville."

"Near your house?"

"Yes. You just can't go anywhere to vote. I can't vote in Newark and you can't vote in Bernardsville. You've got to vote near your home."

"Can we go to your house after we vote?" he asked.

"No, I don't think so because by the time I get you and take you to Bernardsville and then back to Newark, it will be past five o'clock and I told your mom I'd always have you home around six o'clock."

"Oh, that's okay. I'm sure she'd let me stay later," Eddie said. "Maybe we could play some basketball."

"Today there wouldn't be any time for that," I remarked. "Besides, it gets dark around six o'clock during this time of the year."

"Yeah, that's right. By the time we get done with the voting, we will not have any time for basketball. I understand, but when can we play basketball at your house?" he asked.

I knew I was being maneuvered by an eleven-year-old, and I did like to bring Eddie to our house every now and then so I told him we'd vote today, and within the next month, he could come to our house and I would beat him in basketball.

"That's great, Mr. Cooperman. All except you beating me one on one. You'll get beat," Eddie said.

On the way to the voting district, I talked to Eddie about an important special question on the ballot, that of land preservation.

"You'll be able to read about it when we are in the voting booth," I said.

"What do you mean, go into the voting booth? I'm not old enough to vote. How can I go into the voting booth?" Eddie asked.

I explained to Eddie that it would be okay and how I had done this before with my children. He was not convinced and worried people wouldn't let him in. He imagined a scene where he would be embarrassed. He was obviously thinking ahead and didn't want to be rejected. So, I had to assure him it would be okay.

I reiterated that I had done this before and it would be no problem. I told Eddie we would ask the officials at the voting place and they would say yes. I assured him we would not have any problems. "Don't sweat it," I said.

"Okay, but I'm kind of nervous someone will say I can't be there."

I asked him if he were saying that because he's an African American and he was going to a place in my town where almost everyone is going to be white. At this time, Eddie and I were pretty comfortable asking each other questions such as this, so it was no big problem.

"No, it doesn't have anything to do with that," Eddie said. "It's just I don't want to be told in front of a lot of people that I can't go into some place, that's all."

I finally convinced him there would be no embarrassment and we were able to move off that point.

I told Eddie I was concerned that in New Jersey we don't have a lot of woodland where people can walk and a lot of places which I felt should be left as they were without tearing down trees and building houses on them. There was a question on the ballot that had to do with preserving woodland, and I said I was going to vote for it.

Eddie didn't agree with my point of view and asked, "How do you build houses unless you take down the trees?" He pointed to his neighborhood, with few trees, and said the trees were probably cut down so people could live in the buildings. Trees were less important than people and, therefore, expendable.

I tried to take a middle ground and said that Eddie was absolutely right and people do have a right to have good homes and apartments. But, I explained, a lot of people, and I'm one of them, think that we shouldn't take down *all* the trees just so people can put up shopping centers, office buildings and big houses. I said I thought there ought to be some sort of balance between the two.

"Well, I wouldn't worry about that too much. I don't know why you're so interested in trees," Eddie remarked.

"I'm glad you can't vote, Eddie, because you would probably vote against saving the trees," I chuckled. "I thought you liked the trees we saw when we went to the football game."

"They had nice colors, all different colors, but I think homes for people are more important than trees."

"I'm glad I'm doing the voting and not you," I said laughing.

POLLUTION

"Have you learned about pollution in your science class?" I asked.

"Oh, sure. That's when things smell bad and it gets in your lungs and can kill you," he said.

"Yes, that's certainly part of it and we have some regulations, not only for buildings that put bad stuff called pollutants into the air, but cars also have things on them so they don't pollute the air. Sometimes we don't know what we're breathing and it could be pretty harmful. Trees help us in this regard."

I hadn't forgotten our prior conversation and Eddie's position on trees versus houses. I had to make my point about trees carefully!

I found myself getting into the preaching mode about protecting the environment. I explained the reason I always separate things before placing them in the trash can. I told Eddie about recycling and reminded him that when he was at our house, I had showed him that we separated our paper and plastic from soda bottles and tin cans so they can be recycled.

"Uh, huh. I remember you showing me that," said Eddie.

I made my final pollution example when I talked about not throwing things on the ground. I said that it not only looks lousy, but it pollutes the environment just as badly as the gases that leave the smoke stacks in some industrial plants.

On the way to Eddie's home, we drove through our favorite McDonald's and picked up a burger, fries, and orange drink for Eddie. As we continued on to his house, we talked about

Scottie Pippen's worth to the Chicago Bulls and wondered if the NETS would ever win three in a row.

When we pulled up at Eddie's house and said our goodbyes, I noticed that he took his napkin and French fry container, and stuffed them into his plastic cup.

"Atta boy, Eddie. That's cleaning up the car," I said.

"The garbage thing is too small to hold this," he said. Eddie was referring to the small plastic bag that I always put in front of the car for stray pieces of paper, peanuts and fruit pits. "I'll take it with me."

As I pulled away, I glanced in the rearview mirror and as Eddie turned to walk into his house, I saw him pitch the container into the street.

After a wonderful day, I knew he was not doing that in defiance of what I believe, but merely what he sees so many people doing in his neighborhood; simply throwing things onto the sidewalk or into the street. He was careful not to leave debris in my car. He knew how I felt about keeping the car clean. And he always looked for a trash can to put stuff in if we were walking and eating. But, he couldn't make the leap to doing the same thing in his neighborhood. On his home turf, the sidewalk and streets were often the trash can for McDonald's containers.

This is going to be a marathon – there will be no easy victories.

EDDIE'S DREAM II

Eddie at twelve still has a one-track mind concerning basketball.

"You really should be more careful about that style of dribbling," I said.

"What do you mean?"

"That tongue, Eddie. You still keep sticking out that tongue of yours like you are Michael Jordan."

"I know."

"Well, I'm telling you, it's trouble. Someday you are going to trip, fall and bite yourself. Or, someone guarding you will pop you on the chin and your bottom teeth are going to stick right through your tongue. You must close your mouth and keep your teeth together."

"Yeah, I know, Mr. Cooperman. You always say that. But I haven't had an accident yet. And Jordan never bit his tongue off."

"Okay, Eddie – I can't make you keep your tongue in your mouth, but I still think it's dangerous. And I'm going to keep bugging you."

"That's okay. I know you mean well, but it's not the big deal you think it is. When I make the high school team, I'll see if the coach agrees with you."

But, right now there's no coach in Eddie's life who might systematically take him through the basics. There's no consistent adult supervision of the pick-up games that he plays endlessly with various kids who are available. Some weeks he plays with children two or three years younger than he is. Next, he'll compete with someone his own age, and from time to time he might get into a game with older teens that are much bigger, faster, and have more natural talent.

What trips me up, however, is that he continues to think this haphazard, undirected, self-propelled, time-consuming display of street smarts will add up in the future to a possible career in basketball.

Usually when a child is eleven or twelve, as Eddie is now, he is playing in leagues or on his school team. He is learning the fundamentals of the game and the drills to develop good habits. Eddie is learning neither. On one hand, I don't want to sit on his dream, even though I think it is even more unrealistic now than I did two years ago. So we play plenty of basketball, usually a one on one game. Our rules are that I can't rebound offensively, while Eddie can, and I can't shoot closer than ten feet from the basket, while Eddie can.

Even though he is quicker than I am, I'm sixty-three now, it is becoming evident that Eddie has a major problem – the ball doesn't go into the basket with any consistent frequency. The result of this shortcoming is that Eddie's losses are piling up.

"You've got a pretty good jump shot, Mr. Cooperman. That's why you beat me."

"But if you hit your shots, you would win, Eddie."

"I know. I'll have to practice more."

Eddie has a determination and optimism that he will "find his shot" and his basketball future will be bright.

I tried to explain my "domino approach" to his basketball chances. "If you don't make your middle school team, you probably have no chance of making your high school team. And only the top 30 – 40 high school players in the state will be given scholarships to the best basketball colleges. So you must make your middle school team."

Eddie seemed to agree with me. "I see what you mean. The middle school coach will tell the high school coach who the best players are."

"That's right. And more than that, the high school coach will watch the middle school kids practice and play. So, if you don't make the middle school team, you might have to think about something other than basketball."

"But, I am going to make the middle school team."

I know the odds are a million to one that Eddie will play pro basketball. As this dream plays out over the next year or two, I will push him to explore what it might take in the way of preparation to reach other goals. During our last visit he said he might want to be a cop, "if I don't make the pros". Finally, an alternative.

Right now, this doesn't have to be a source of contention for us. But I know that if he doesn't do certain fundamental things in school within the next few years, he will be closing all sorts of doors that could lead to future successes. And I know I can't let him decide without trying to influence him because how he spends his time will dictate one future or another. And no one who loves a child should ever let that youngster choose the satisfactions of a whim over the long-term advantages of a piece by piece game plan that could lead to a variety of possible long range goals.

I will ask Eddie if he has made his middle school team next year. If he hasn't, I will cut back on our basketball playing and gently start to remove the idea of his becoming a pro. Mugsey Bouges is not reality.

This may sound a bit manipulative, but most adults walk a tightrope. We never want to destroy a child's dream; in fact we should encourage it. Some of us may even feel our children have the ability to be a future president. However, as the children grow, reality sets in and there are signs at age five or ten that maybe someone else's child will be contending for the presidency or for the point guard position on a professional basketball team.

THE ELEPHANT STORY

Eddie has asked me about stealing. He was having a slice of pizza at a restaurant.

"What do you think would happen if I took these salt shakers?"

"Why would you want to take the salt shakers, Eddie?"

"I don't mean I would. I just mean *if* I took them. I could put them in my pocket and no one would notice. Then, what would happen?"

"You're right. You'd probably be able to get away with it and you'd be able to steal the salt shakers. But, what are you driving at?"

"I know some older boys who take things from the supermarket and from some stores and they haven't been caught. They say it's easy and the store isn't going to miss them anyway. I don't think that's right, but I just wondered what you thought."

"You really don't have to ask that, Eddie," I said. "If it's someone else's property, it's not yours and you don't have any right to it. You wouldn't want someone stealing your bike or your basketball, would you?"

"No, I wouldn't. But this is different because they're stealing it from a big store that has plenty more things."

"No. That's not right. The store had to pay someone for the product it put on the shelf. The owner has a right to sell that product and make a profit, not to have someone steal from him.

Besides," I added, "sooner or later, the thieves will get caught and then be tried for theft."

"Will they go to jail?" Eddie asked.

"If the person is under eighteen and it's the first time, probably not. But if he steals again he ultimately might have to spend time in a juvenile home, which is kind of like a jail."

"Oh, I don't think I'd like being in a place like that."

"So, perhaps you were thinking about stealing something. Am I right?"

"No. I was just wondering because it seems a lot of older boys are doing it and they aren't going to jail."

The conversation ended and a couple of weeks later while we were sitting under a tree having a soda, I asked Eddie if he ever heard the story of the teenage elephants. He kind of smiled and thought it was going to be a joke. When he said he had not heard the story, I began to tell it to him.

"It seems there were way too many elephants in one part of Africa and they needed to move part of the herd to another place where there were no elephants. Since it's illegal now to kill any elephants, they decided to move about fifty elephants to a place far away. They figured the older ones and the babies wouldn't be able to manage so long a journey and they decided to take the teenage elephants for the journey because they were young and strong."

Eddie began to smile, thinking this was going to be one of my silly jokes. But he continued to listen.

"Anyhow, they rounded up fifty of the elephants and marched them off over the mountains and through the flatland.

There was no problem along the way as to what they would eat. There was plenty of food and a lot of water to drink. So they got along reasonably well."

By this time Eddie figured out that this wasn't going to be a joke and he asked, "So, did they make it?"

"What do you think happened?"

"I don't know. Maybe they just sat down and stopped. Or maybe they got there all right."

"They did make it to where they were going, and for a while everything was okay. But then they started having trouble with one or two of the elephants. These elephants knocked down a big fence and one charged into a house and just broke it apart. Another started to uproot trees that most elephants never bothered with. Anyway, the game wardens who brought them thought they had a couple of bad elephants, just like a bad apple in a group of good apples. And so they captured the worst elephants and took them away from the rest."

"Did that help? Was everything okay then?" Eddie asked.

"Not for very long. Later that week, another elephant really went nuts. There was a jeep with some tourists on it, and they wanted to see some animals of Africa. They were just sitting there when this elephant ran into the jeep, flipped it over, and hurt some of the people."

"Oh, man!" Eddie exclaimed. "Then what? What happened?" he urged.

"Well, when a bad elephant does things like that, they sometimes have to shoot the elephant."

"Shoot him? I thought you said they couldn't shoot elephants and that's why they were moving them."

"Well, this one was really a bad elephant who had gone wild. He probably was going to kill someone if they just left him around," I offered.

"But why can't they do something else? All he did was flip over a car. That's not reason for killing an elephant."

I was tempted at this time to move the conversation from a bad elephant to a bad kid, but somehow I resisted.

"They put this elephant in a place all by himself. But, by then the Game Warden was getting really upset. So he called in some elephant experts, the best people in Africa, to figure out what was going wrong."

"That seems pretty smart," said Eddie. "Just killing the elephants didn't seem to make any sense to me."

"Anyway, the experts came in and hung out with the elephants for almost a week, day and night. They watched the elephants and after a week, the experts said they had the problem solved. They knew exactly what was wrong."

"Okay. What was it?"

"They said that when teenage elephants are growing up, they need to have all kinds of other elephants around. The expert figured that the teenage elephants needed to see the way the little elephants did dumb things and sometimes exposed themselves to danger and the way the older elephants would protect them. They also needed to see how the older elephants acted so they could learn from them and not make stupid mistakes. The older elephants could also show the young ones not to misbehave and get in trouble."

"So that was the problem. The young teenage elephants didn't have any older and younger elephants around to see what was being done. When one elephant did something wrong, the other elephants followed what it was doing. And since some of the bad elephants seemed to be getting away with it, the others thought they could get away with it also."

Eddie was quiet for a moment. Then he asked one of the first adult questions in our relationship. "Then you think sometimes kids are doing bad things 'cause they never saw someone set good examples for them?"

"Could be. It sure does make you think about it, doesn't it?"

"Yes. It makes me wonder," Eddie admitted.

This simple story became a breakthrough. Eddie came back to the elephant story several times during the next few months and this launched some conversation about right and wrong and who determines the difference.

HI, MY NAME IS....

I wanted Eddie to understand that getting a good job requires skills and many African American men have paid the price to acquire these skills. I say this because most of the African American men Eddie sees don't work, and he continues to feel the deck is stacked against him and that he doesn't have a chance.

I thought it would be stilted if I took Eddie to see some of the African American people I know. He would probably feel the scenario was too programmed. I was having a tough time figuring out how to make my point in a natural setting.

One day in McDonald's I saw a fiftyish African American man in a coat and tie munching on a burger. Without hesitation I said to Eddie, "Let's talk to that man over there."

Before he could resist or even stammer a reply, we were in front of the man. "Hi," I said cheerily. "My name is Saul Cooperman and this is Eddie."

The man was startled, but saw we were no threat and managed a weak smile. "I'm Eddie's mentor, and I've been trying to impress upon him the necessity to do well in school and make the connection between school and a good job; that sort of thing."

As I was finishing my comment, the man responded with a light up the world grin and said, "Young man, your mentor knows what he is talking about. I'm an accountant, and I had to study hard to get where I am today." He went on for several minutes while Eddie responded with "Uh, huh" or "yes" when asked if he understood.

Maybe I was just lucky with the accountant, but I resolved to try the drill again. I sought out well-dressed African American men and approached them. Eddie wasn't thrilled about my caper, but conversation between us convinced him that these situations were unrehearsed, and he was interested in what the men said. At least he seemed so.

During the next month, we met a lawyer and a sales manager. Both of them talked with enthusiasm about their work and the studying they had to do to get their jobs.

But, the best person we talked to was the manager of the McDonald's. I had seen this man for months organizing and directing the people of his establishment. He didn't meet the coat and tie test, but he seemed to be someone who was going to be successful at whatever he did. He had pizzazz.

I introduced myself and Eddie and then listened.

"I started out in another McDonald's when I was a senior in high school. My first job was making French fries. Now, ten years later, I'm managing my own store."

He told Eddie what inventory was. He talked about the special programs, keeping the books and the rules and regulations concerning hiring. "In all these things, I had to be able to read and understand to do my job well. If I didn't understand math, I'd be fired in a minute. Studying is the difference between making French fries like that kid back there and managing this place."

I felt like standing up and cheering. If I wrote what I wanted him to say, I couldn't have done as well.

Eddie seemed impressed. He asked a few questions, and we discussed how the man became a manager on the way home. The lawyer, accountant, and sales manager were impressive, but their jobs were remote for a boy who was twelve. McDonald's was real.

EDDIE'S BIKE

Any kid who has owned a bike knows there's a lot more to that bike than just riding it. All this came home to me one day when I spoke with Eddie, and he told me his bike had a serious problem.

He said his bike was broken. He had let a couple of his friends ride the bike and one friend jumped off the curb and somehow broke the brakes. Now his mom wouldn't let him ride it while it was broken, and he didn't know how to fix it.

I asked if anyone else looked at the bike and he said they did but "nobody knows how to fix it". He was discouraged and didn't see any way out of the dilemma. When I said I would take a look at it, he was overjoyed.

"Thanks, Mr. Cooperman," he said. His optimism oozed out at once, thinking that perhaps I could fix the problem. Little did he know that I have trouble fixing anything and when it comes time to doing handyman chores around the house, my wife, Paulette, is usually the one who gets the call. While I'm pretty good at painting and gardening, if it has anything to do with screwdrivers, drills, wrenches and hammers, I'm not too swift. But, I thought I'd give it a try.

I told him I would be down around noon. I said that after looking at the bike, we would go to a shopping mall, something we had planned to do.

"Can I ride my bike a bit after you fix it?" asked Eddie.

"I said I'd *try* to fix it, Eddie. I'll do my best. I'll see you on Saturday."

When I got off the phone, Paulette looked at me and said, "*You're* going to fix the bike?"

Before I could answer, a big grin crossed her face and she burst out laughing. I started laughing, too. In truth, we both knew it wasn't likely I'd be able to fix the bike. But I said to her, "Maybe I'll get lucky. Maybe it's simple and only needs a tightening of a screw or a nut."

When I arrived at his house, Eddie had the bike right in the middle of the living room floor, already turned upside down, waiting for the expert eye of a seasoned handyman. I'm sure he thought that a few minutes of deft, effortless gestures would be sufficient. Throughout the years, Eddie had grown to think that I knew a lot about many subjects. I told him it just seemed like a lot because I was older. This didn't work and he said, "Don't forget you said, after you fix the bike, I could go for a ride before we visit the shopping center."

I'm in for it now. He really believes I can fix this.

Eddie explained how the brake didn't work and the clamps didn't stop the tires. When I traced the wire from the handlebars to the tires, I could see there was far too much slack in it to be safe.

I could also see that the pad connected to the end of the bike was not being pulled close enough to the metal to stop the tire from turning. There were only two or three nuts between the brakes on the handlebar and the pads on the tire. Surely, if I turned these one way or the other, I would fix it. One of my wrenches fit one of the nuts and another adjustable wrench fit another one. I turned the nuts various ways but nothing happened. I was running true to form. I was not about to get lucky and make the repair.

"Hey, Eddie, how long has your tire been this worn?"

"Huh?"

"The tire. Feel how smooth it is."

"Oh, yeah, it's an old tire."

"But it's not safe either," I said.

"What do you mean?"

"When a car or bike has really old tires, the treads get worn off and it goes bald. Then it becomes a safety problem."

Eddie didn't hear my last comment. "Bald?" Eddie laughed, running fingers across the top of his very close cropped hair.

"Yeah, BALD," I replied, while reaching out and patting his head in mock imitation of his own gesture. We both cracked up.

I left the condition of the tire and returned to the major problem, the brake. I admitted I couldn't fix it and said that we had to take it to a bike shop. I said I didn't understand the problem and even if I had, I wasn't sure my wrenches would work on it, and I was concerned about the bald tire. I suggested we put the bike in the back of my car and find the nearest place to get it fixed.

Off we went to drive a couple of miles to a place where Eddie's mom bought the bike one winter. We parked, went in, and found the owner, a fiftyish-year-old Korean man, talking to his assistant, a young black man in his twenties.

While we were waiting, Eddie said quietly, "That black guy seems to know how to fix bikes; I've been watching him work."

"How do you think he learned?" I asked Eddie.

He thought for a few seconds and said, "Maybe he learned from that old guy," he said pointing to the Korean gentleman.

"I think you might be right. But, maybe he took a course in some vocational school."

I then did something that often made Eddie uncomfortable, I approached the black man who was working on a bike and asked him how he learned to repair bikes.

"I swept the floor and would clean this place when I was a teen. After I graduated from Orange High School, Mr. J asked me if I wanted a job. I've been here ever since, and I'm twenty-seven now. All I know, he taught me."

Eddie nodded but said nothing. I was about to say something about hard work paying off but the owner approached us and asked how he could help. I explained the situation to the owner, and he assured me it would be easily resolved. Eddie, of course, wanted to watch. Very few mechanical things interest me, but I wanted to see what he would do that I didn't. Unbeknownst to me, there was another nut that I hadn't seen, and with a couple of turns with the appropriate wrench, the brake was miraculously fixed.

I asked the owner if he had a used tire, which was better than the one that Eddie had. I really debated with myself as to whether or not I should buy Eddie a tire. I always go through this struggle. Mentoring is not supposed to be a process where the mentor is forever buying things for a child. God knows, he could use a lot of things, but then it is expected, and that becomes the focus of your relationship, rather than values and the building of a child's character. So, after looking at the front tire, which was in reasonable shape, I asked the owner if he had a used one, something like it.

"Yes, I think I do, from another bike that got a new tire. I'd be glad to put that one on for you."

The procedure was done quickly, I paid $10, and we left with a better tire and brakes that worked.

I didn't have to prompt Eddie to thank both the owner and the assistant for repairing the bike and giving us the tire for what seemed to be a bargain-basement price. As I left the bike shop, it occurred to me that there would be several lessons in this for Eddie.

He had learned, for instance, that taking care of your possessions is important, and if you can't take care of them yourself, you have to spend money to have them fixed. He also learned that you have to know where to go to have things done right. And he saw the owner and apprentice had specific skills and were paid for what they knew. And even though Eddie thinks I'm a bright guy, he saw that I didn't have a clue as to how to fix the bike, but other people did. And finally he had another lesson in race relations. He saw an elderly Asian man and a young black man working side by side.

I felt pretty good about the way things had turned out. I told him to ride the bike down to the car and try it out and make sure he tried the brakes. He zoomed down the block and I caught up to him where the car was parked.

"So, how does it feel?"

"Oh, great now, Mr. Cooperman. It's all fixed and rides great. And thanks again for getting the bike fixed, even if you didn't fix it."

It was clear from his tone that he wasn't ribbing me; he meant every word he said. I know in the mentoring relationship the child is supposed to benefit from the older person's experience and guidance, but, I, too, was benefiting from this friendship. Eddie realized I didn't "know everything," and I was fallible, but that was okay. He was starting to see that people of different races could respect and work with each other, as the Korean proprietor and his African American assistant vividly demonstrated.

I had three main goals for Eddie, and they became clearer to me as the months went by. First and foremost, I wanted to help develop a young man that had good values and good character. Second, I wanted to see that he developed a work ethic which would enable him to see things through and take pride in his work, and, third, I wanted to be there when he walked down the aisle at his high school graduation.

As I drove back to Bernardsville late in the day, I felt good about our relationship, and I felt good about Eddie. He was honest; didn't associate with bad kids, and was starting to see there was some connection between getting a good job and working hard. Academics were another thing but, on balance, things were looking up!

REST IN PEACE

"Did he die?"

"Is he still alive?"

When I first heard these questions from Eddie, he was only eight. But, now he's twelve and the question persists. At first I used to say to him, "Why do you always ask are they alive?" Then I realized how dumb my question was. Eddie has seen death close up. He knows people who have died young, others who have died from AIDS, or many who died because they were "in the wrong place at the wrong time" and were killed accidentally.

It doesn't make any difference whether I talk about someone who is a basketball player, or whether it's an associate of mine that Eddie met while visiting the office. He will often say something like, "Mr. Jensen, the man we saw at the picnic last year, I remember him. Is he still alive?"

I once heard Eddie say, "If I graduate from high school…" I mentioned to him that if he worked hard, of course he would graduate from high school.

"No, no. That's not what I meant, Mr. Cooperman. I meant, if I live long enough to graduate from high school."

****

A few weeks ago, a friend of mine came to play hoops with Eddie and his friend, Keith. It was two on two, the young black kids against the old white guys. About a month later, I mentioned my friend in conversation and Eddie said, true to form, "Is he still alive?" He was just unable to imagine people he met not being subject to the life and death roulette of inner city life.

I tried to put myself in his shoes. If I thought I might not make it to eighteen, why all the fuss about reading and getting a good job? It was hard for me to accept his thinking, but I had to respect it and deal with it.

FATHER'S DAY

In the life of any youngster, some days are always going to be more important than others. New Year's Day is rarely as special as a child's own birthday. For some families, Columbus Day or Valentines Day has special meaning. Others place greater emphasis on Hanukkah or Christmas, but for almost all kids, there's a particular kick to Mother's Day and Father's Day.

Such holidays, of course, can be all the more upsetting for those who've suffered the loss of a parent to early death. And there's a unique void in the hearts of children, like Eddie, who do not have a relationship with their fathers. Eddie's mother is there for him as often as a single mom can be. But his father, whose absence is as conspicuous as it is painful, is seldom there.

I must admit that I struggle with my feelings for Eddie's real dad. I recently asked my young friend what made him sad.

"Sad?" he questioned.

"You know. Like what almost makes you want to cry?"

"Nothing," he answered flatly.

"Nothing ever?" I asked persistently.

"Well, my dad came to see me last month."

"Shouldn't that make you happy?" I asked.

"No way," said Eddie, "he never came to see me when I was little, and now he comes around to show his face and he only lives ten minutes from us."

"But maybe he's trying, Eddie," I said. "Maybe he had reasons why he couldn't see you." Although I can't imagine what the reasons might be that would keep a father from seeing his son, my motive is to try to get father and son together.

"He tried to tell me about money. Why is he telling me this? I don't want to know it. I gave him my 'mad face' and he went away. You understand, don't you, Mr. Cooperman?"

"Yes. I guess I see what you mean, Eddie. But, people change. Maybe he's changed, and you could give him a chance."

Eddie didn't respond. He will probably think about what I have said, but clearly he is terribly hurt by his father's absence and doesn't want to open himself up to be hurt even more. If misery loves company, many of Eddie's friends are in the same situation, with fathers "not in the picture." But, that doesn't make Eddie's pain any less.

In May of 1998, Eddie's shop class in school was given the choice of either making checkerboards for their own use or Father's Day plaques. Eddie spent time cutting, sanding, polishing, and then carving a "Happy Father's Day" inscription on the wooden plaque that his teacher provided. His was, as they say, a labor of love.

"Mr. Cooperman, I have something for you."

When I opened it and saw the wooden plaque, I was speechless.

I stammered, "Are you sure this is for me?"

"Sure, I'm sure," he said. "You like it?"

"I love it, Eddie – thank you so much for making it for me."

On my ride home, I was so sad thinking of this little guy making the Father's Day plaque. Maybe he didn't want the other kids to know his father seldom saw him. But, then again, most of his friends didn't have fathers in their lives so his situation wasn't unusual. No, he wanted to give *me* this, rather than make a checkerboard.

Oh, Eddie, I thought, life is not easy for you. I love my plaque, yet I wish someone else was receiving it. I wish Eddie and his dad could be closer, but I have to agree with Eddie – where was he? Why wasn't he with Eddie more when he was one; why wasn't he with him when he was five, or six, or seven? Why?

I could be the greatest sponsor in the world for him, the finest, and most generous of benefactors. It still wouldn't put back into his life what has been taken by the one adult who could have mattered, the one adult who should have been at those birthday parties; the single male who ought to have taught this kid to jump, run, dribble, spit, joke, pray and appreciate himself as a beautiful boy.

And I hate that – I really do.

THE CHINESE RESTAURANT

Eddie and I had been talking about going to a "fancy restaurant" for some time. He said he was still nervous because he still wasn't sure about using a knife and fork to cut things.

I knew this would be a problem, even though we had practiced on French fries at McDonald's. I assured Eddie he was doing much better, and he would do just fine.

We decided to go to a restaurant at 5:00 PM because it would be relatively uncrowded at that time, and we could get a table in a corner. Eddie said that he had once had Chinese food and liked it, so we went to a restaurant in West Orange.

The waiter escorted us to our seat and Eddie remembered to take the napkin and to put it in his lap.

When the menu came, I asked him, "Eddie, can you read this? I'm having trouble with it."

"I can't read that. What is that writing, Mr. Cooperman?"

"I was just kidding you. That's in Chinese, and I can't read it either. But, there is an English translation next to it."

"Oh, yeah, I see it now. But I don't know what all these things mean. What's this 'Moo Goo Gai Pan'? That sounds crazy."

I wanted him to hear the waiter explain what it was, so I said, "I'm not exactly sure what it is, let's ask the waiter."

"I really don't want anything that sounds so strange. Isn't there anything that you know I would like?"

"Why don't you try these fried noodle twists that are on the table? You dip them into this sauce; I think you'll like it."

Eddie picked up some of the noodles, dipped them into the duck sauce, and tentatively began to chew on one. He then popped another into his mouth. "Boy, this stuff is good. I really like this."

He proceeded to make short work of them before the waiter came back. He explained what Moo Goo Gai Pan was, as well as Moo Shu Chicken. I ordered an egg roll for Eddie, wonton soup, and some Moo Shu Chicken.

I was right on the egg roll, and Eddie loved it.

"Boy, this stuff is good. I've never had anything like this before, but I like the taste."

"Fantastic! You liked the fried noodle twists and the egg roll, now why don't you try the soup, and if you like it, fine. Otherwise, I'll eat it."

He dipped into the soup, buoyed by his apparent like of the egg roll. But I knew when it immediately reached his taste buds; he didn't like it at all.

"This is nasty, Mr. Cooperman. How could anyone like this?"

So I finished the soup and waited for the Moo Shu Chicken.

The waiter went through the routine of lifting the chicken and vegetables from the plate and onto the pancake and, with quick expertise, folded them and presented one to Eddie and one to me.

"What do you do with it now?" he asked.

"You pick it up and eat it just like you're eating a hotdog; bite one end of it and see how it tastes."

Eddie proceeded to pick up the Moo Shu Chicken and took a large bite. Big mistake! Panic seized his face and I knew this was not going to go down easily.

"I can see you don't like it, Eddie. But, if you can, just swallow it."

And, with a Herculean effort, he managed to swallow one bite of Moo Shu Chicken. He would not be returning for a second bite.

"Now, that is really terrible, Mr. Cooperman. That's worse than the soup."

"Well, I'm going to eat my Moo Shu Chicken, and then I might have another one. You can take yours home if you'd like. Perhaps your mom or Duane would like the other one."

"Oh, my mom will like that. She likes most things."

"Okay, we'll ask the waiter to put it in a bag for us."

"How are we going to make the other one (the waiter hadn't done it) so we can take it home? Should we call the waiter back?" Eddie asked.

"No, let's try it ourselves. It's not really hard. Why don't you take the chicken and vegetables and put them in the pancake and then we can try to remember how the waiter folded it over."

We did this with ease and Eddie was quite proud of his ability to fold the pancake.

After we had left the restaurant, Eddie asked me about Chinese people.

"I don't see many Chinese people. Are there many Chinese people in America?"

"No, not too many. You usually find Chinese people in major cities like New York, Chicago, Atlanta or San Francisco," I said. "But there are a lot of Chinese people in the world. Do you know, Eddie, that almost one out of every five people in the whole world is Chinese?"

"Nah, you're kidding me again. Why do you say things like that?"

"Well, it's true. Sometimes I do try to make jokes, but this is the truth. China is a very large country, and there are one and a quarter billion Chinese people in China and the rest of the world. There are only six billion people in the whole world so you can see that almost one out of every five people in the world is Chinese."

"I didn't know that."

"Well, there's lots of stuff to learn in the world and that's why it's so important to read because then you learn all about this stuff."

"Yeah, well, I've been trying to make better grades in school this year. I haven't gotten any papers back, but I haven't missed any days yet."

"That's fantastic, Eddie. I hope you're able to keep that up."

Three weeks later, the report cards came out. His attendance was much better but there were no B's in English, math, science, or social studies. In fact, the three D's and one C were no improvement at all. Obviously, there would be no restaurant, movie or $20 reward for B's in English and Math.

I resolved, however, to keep whatever pressure on Eddie that I could. He listens to me and often tells me what I said a month or a year later. I know I have some influence on his behavior. But, academics is still a tough nut to crack.

SUMMER 2000

I was talking with Celie about plans for the summer and asked her if she had given any thought to Eddie's summer. It was particularly important because she had just begun a job at a neighborhood pre-school program. I knew she was going to work from 12:00 noon to 6:00 PM, and, therefore, would not be available to supervise Eddie's whereabouts. And Eddie is thirteen now, and his horizons are expanding.

"I think I'm going to enroll him in the summer playground program. The kids have to be there at 9:00 in the morning. They're provided lunch and they leave at 3:00 PM. He'll go right home and stay at home until I return at 6:00 PM."

I mentioned that that seemed like a good plan, but wondered if they were going to do anything for Eddie's problems in reading and writing. I broached the subject with Celie and asked her if they would be doing anything to help Eddie in those subjects.

When she said that it was mostly recreation and wouldn't have much to do with reading and math, I asked her if she would mind if I tried to find out if there's a program in the area that might help him with his reading. She readily agreed.

I knew someone who ran a summer program at the Bessie Green Learning Center in Newark and I asked him if we could get Eddie into the program. I knew they stressed reading, writing, and mathematics from 9:00 AM – 3:00 PM, Monday through Thursday, with Friday being devoted to a field trip that had something to do with what the kids were studying. I talked with Celie about the program and she was most enthusiastic.

"That would be really good because he would be in school until 3:00 PM, and he wouldn't take the bus home until 3:30

PM, so he would only have a couple of hours at home before I got there." she said.

I asked her to think it over for a couple of days and let me know if she still felt that way.

"I don't need to think it over. I'd like to do it," she said. "Eddie, get in here. I want to talk with you."

Eddie came in and Celie said, "Mr. Cooperman knows of a program at the Bessie Green Learning Center. You'll be able to work on your reading and writing from Monday through Thursday and then go on a field trip on Fridays. I'm going to get you enrolled in that program," she stated.

"Eddie, what do you think of that? Does that seem okay with you?" I asked.

"It's okay, I guess," he said.

I asked Celie if we could just step outside and talk for a moment. When we were outside, I said, "He doesn't seem too enthusiastic and if he sees this as a punishment, I don't think this is going to work. What do you think?"

"I'm not giving him the opportunity to make any decisions. I'm making the decision for him, and he's going to that school," she said.

I respected her strength to want to do the right thing for her child, but I also thought there would be some problems with Eddie in attending Bessie Green. These concerns came to pass when Eddie missed six of the first fifteen sessions. I talked with Celie about his absences.

"He's got stomach problems, Mr. Cooperman. He says he didn't feel well."

"Well, it's interesting to me that he didn't have any of the stomach problems on the three Fridays when they went on the field trips. He only had problems when they were focusing on the reading, writing, and math," I remarked.

"We've been through this before," she said somewhat annoyed, "you don't believe that he had stomach problems. Well, I believe him. He just wasn't feeling well."

A brick wall! I really like Celie, but on this one we are at odds. She believes his stomach ache routine and so he will keep using it. I have little leverage on this, but I'm sure Celie understands my point that the learning center wasn't doing him much good if he was absent so much of the time.

During the next twenty sessions, Eddie only missed three, still three too many but maybe Celie was tightening up on the stomach problems. Two weeks before the end of the summer school, and with Celie's permission, I met with his teachers.

They told me he seldom concentrated, and although he caused no problems and sometimes enjoyed the assignments, he was reading below grade level and his math skills were poor. I asked if I could have the results of the standardized tests that they were giving at the end of the summer school, and the teachers said they would provide me with them.

Two weeks later, I showed Eddie the good news that he had improved in both reading and math. Some of the learning stuck and he had progressed. However, he was still quite a bit below average for his age and grade level.

I decided, initially, to accentuate the positive and pointed to the progress he made in reading and math.

"Yeah, but it still says I'm not doing well. Can they keep me back?"

I explained this was a summer program and he was already promoted to the eighth grade. I said what they were saying was that he had improved, but still had a long way to go.

"Yes, but I'm doing better, and I'm going to do better next year. I'm really going to focus," Eddie said with some enthusiasm.

I spoke sternly to Eddie, "I've heard you say that now for four years and the results are always the same – mostly D's, a C here and there, and once in a while an F. I'm not convinced that you're going to do better. You know it's going to be much harder because the eighth grade books will be difficult."

I told Eddie I wouldn't discuss the specifics with his mom, but she had to know that the problems in reading and math still persisted. He said he understood, but obviously he wasn't happy with it.

I thought that if his mom knew what the score was, she'd make sure he did his homework every night. At least I hoped so. I told Eddie I wished I could be standing over him each day, and explained that although I knew he wouldn't like that, I'd make sure his homework was completed and done right. But, I said, since I can't be there, I'll try to get his mom to see that he does his homework.

I talked to Celie about Eddie's work at Bessie Green and told her that the teacher said he didn't always work hard and he wasn't reading at grade level.

"He's reading at grade level, Mr. Cooperman. I've had him read all the words," she said.

I didn't expect this.

"He might be able to say the words, but he doesn't always understand what they mean. Saying the words is one thing, but knowing what they mean is another."

"I see what you mean," she said. "And, he doesn't use the dictionary you bought him. It just sits there."

"Neither you nor I can make Eddie look up words in the dictionary," I said, "but, he's got to understand more words so he can deal with the more difficult work in the eighth grade."

"Well, I'll do my best to make sure he does his homework every night," Celie commented.

I thanked her for her genuine sincerity and told her that if she is pushing him at home and I keep asking him questions about what he's doing in school, perhaps just to get us off his back, he'll do better work. If he gets B's instead of D's, I said, he might actually be proud of what he's doing.

But, after I momentarily became hopeful, a sobering thought set in.

Celie was concerned.

I was concerned.

But Eddie was not concerned.

Doing well in school was not something that was important to Eddie.

I had to face the facts.

I had tried many ways to get Eddie to work hard and achieve academically. None had succeeded. I knew myself, and I would never stop trying to get Eddie to want to read and do well. But the reality was that at age thirteen, he hadn't seen the light.

I will keep pounding my message, but this is starting to look hopeless.

HIGH STAKES TEST

In New Jersey, children must pass a "high stakes" test in order to receive a diploma. This test is given in the eleventh grade and children who fail it are given three more chances to pass it before the end of their senior year. Because so much rides on this, the state gives a test in the eighth grade that is a good predictor of success on the eleventh grade test. Called the GEPA (grade eight proficiency assessment) children who do poorly on it are put in remedial classes so that they can learn what they should have mastered in prior years.

I had asked Celie and Eddie in June of 2001 if they had received the results of the GEPA. Celie said she had not received anything from the school and Eddie said he thought it was to be mailed. In July, the results had not arrived and I asked Celie if she would sign a letter giving me permission to get the results from the school. She readily agreed.

"Eddie, do you want to come with me?" I asked.

"Sure," he replied cheerfully.

On the way to the school, we talked about the GEPA and its importance. "I know it is important, Mr. Cooperman. The teachers kept telling me about it. I really tried my best and I think I did okay but the math was hard." After some bureaucratic dead ends, we found a very capable guidance counselor's secretary who found Eddie's scores and put them in an envelope. Eddie was eager to see the results and wanted to open the envelope in the school office. "Let's go outside," I said, "we can sit on a bench and no one will bother us." We found a quiet place under a tree, and Eddie opened the envelope, looked at it for a few seconds and quietly said, "I don't think I did too well in math."

The results were divided into English, reading, and math; and each of the major subject areas were further broken into sub-sections. Eddie had quickly grasped the situation. He had done an average job on the reading, and while his English skills were below average, he probably wouldn't be placed in a remedial class.

The math was something else. His highest score in one of the sub-sections placed Eddie in the 40th percentile, and the other sub-sections were between the 10th percentile and the 30th percentile. The results were also displayed in bar graph format and the results were devastating to Eddie. For the first time I saw him very upset, as his jaw dropped and he kept saying, "I didn't think I did that badly. You know I've been studying. What am I going to do?" I saw no need to review each sub-section in detail; Eddie got the point.

I was thinking about what I wanted to say when Eddie continued, "I can't see why math is so important; it doesn't seem fair that I couldn't graduate just because I don't know about a circle or a triangle. It just seems so stupid. I've been working hard at math and I thought I would do much better," he said.

"Math is important, Eddie, and we've talked about this so much. You may not have to know the degrees in a triangle, but you sure as heck are going to be using math every day in your life and you know it. Remember when we were going to Bradley Beach last summer and I asked you to figure out how long it would take us to get there if we averaged so many miles an hour? It might be important to know how long it will take you to get some place, and to do it you've got to know math. Or the time we were trying to decide whether the bananas or the apples were cheaper? Since you like both, it would pay to buy what is cheaper. Math! And the time we had to decide to stay or leave when we were waiting for the boat in Verona Park? Remember that?"

"I do," he said. "It's just hard for me. I was embarrassed when I couldn't figure out the car payments when we were in the new car place. But, some of it is stupid, like trying to find the next number when they give you four or five numbers. I thought I was doing better. I think I got all the fractions right."

He was obviously hurt and his mind was jumping around in a haphazard way. Rather than start a discussion on sequences I went back to his statement that math was hard for him. "Sure math is difficult for you, Eddie; there are many things that will be hard for you, and this is one of them. If you don't do better, you won't make it through high school; it's as simple as that."

I thought that confronting the issue head on was the only way to handle it. I tempered these remarks with, "We can continue to work on math. You will have to work hard, but you can do it. You have made progress in the last few months, even though the GEPA results weren't good."

A few days later, without Eddie's knowledge, I met with his high school principal. (Eddie had been promoted to ninth grade and was scheduled for remedial math.) I asked the principal if he could arrange for Eddie's math teacher to give him some extra help after school a few days each week. I thought by meeting with the principal in the summer Eddie might have an advantage in the upcoming school year. My plans came to a screeching halt, as the principal said, "In a more perfect world, all our math teachers would tutor kids after school. But, some of these kids are very difficult in class and at the end of the day, the teachers just want to go home, and I really can't blame them. And, even if I required them to work after school, the union contract says they have to stay after school for only fifteen minutes. Not much you can accomplish in that time." He seemed like a good man who hadn't given up, but there wasn't much I was going to get from him or the school.

I talked with my daughter Suzanne, who had taught eighth graders for twelve years, hoping to get some ideas from her. She looked through her stacks of books and came upon a book *Help Yourself in Math*. The book stated a problem, like most books, but would then give a step-by-step analysis on the way to solve the problem. After explaining the problem, it would give similar problems, and then detail the correct way to solve them. Perhaps Eddie could work at his own pace when I was not with him. Since I saw him only once each week, he would have to take responsibility and the book would serve as a self-guide. I thanked Suzanne, and was excited about the prospects.

For two weeks he said nothing about math, and I kept my mouth shut, as hard as that was for me to do. The week before school was to begin, he brought up the subject. "Mr. Cooperman, I was just thinking, maybe you could help me with my math homework again. Would you do that for me?" He had made a specific suggestion, and I didn't want to squash it in any way. But, he was still so far behind; his ninth grade math seemed like a foreign language. There was so much he still did not know.

"Eddie, you saw the results of the GEPA; if you are to learn what you must know, we have to go back to some basic stuff. What we have been doing – multiplication and division, understanding decimals and fractions – is fourth grade stuff. I'm sorry to say this to you, but you have to know where you are and the job ahead." I showed him Suzanne's book, and indicated where he was and what ninth grade math was like.

"I understand," Eddie said, "What can I do? Will you help me?"

"I will, Eddie, I will."

By November, we were starting to work on simple problems, such as "David had $5 and needs to buy eight bananas. The eight bananas weigh two pounds and bananas cost $.45 a pound. How much change should David get?"

We kept at this for several weeks.

ANNE FRANK

While we were walking by a store, Eddie saw some Christmas decorations and remembered that I didn't celebrate Christmas.

"What holiday do you have, Mr. Cooperman?" Eddie asked.

"Jewish people celebrate a holiday called Hanukkah," I said.

"What's that about?" asked Eddie.

I told him the story had to do with a war between Jewish people and another nation that wanted to destroy the Jews. Part of the story has to do with oil that was used to light a lamp and it was only supposed to last one day, but somehow it lasted for eight days. So, Jewish people celebrate this holiday by lighting eight candles.

"I just learned in my school that there were some people called Nazis, who wanted to kill Jewish people," said Eddie.

This led to a discussion of why Adolf Hitler wanted to kill all Jewish people.

****

Eddie was still upset by Hitler's final solution. He couldn't understand why they would want to kill little kids or old people. He said that his teacher told them about a young girl who wrote about what was going on but she was killed. Eddie wanted to deal with the specifics of the murder of a young girl rather than the concept of scapegoating.

"I think that she died, but somebody found her book."

"Oh," I said, "you must be talking about *The Diary of Anne Frank*.

"Yes, that's her name. That's the name the teacher said," said Eddie.

I told Eddie about Anne Frank and how her family lived and that she ultimately was killed, but her diary was discovered, and her words were translated into many languages and millions of people have read her book. Seizing the moment, I asked Eddie if he would like to read about Anne Frank.

He was quiet for several moments and said nothing. Finally he remarked, "I just can't understand why anyone would want to kill children. That's just not right," he said.

The conversation appeared to be over, and we got into my car and drove to a field where we tossed around a football, commenting on each other's inability to throw a good spiral or to catch every ball that the other person threw.

After about thirty minutes of running around the field with Eddie, I was tired and said, "I think that's enough for today. I'm thirsty. Would you like to get something to drink?"

"That would be great, but I want to ask you if there's anyone who still kills Jewish people, especially little kids and old people?"

Instead of answering directly, I brought up the question of Anne Frank again.

"Would you want me to read some of Anne Frank's diary to you?" I asked. "I could read some and you could read some more."

"Oh, yes. I sure would. Would you do that?" he asked. He was uneasy when I wanted him to read a book, but when I said I would read some of it, he jumped at the suggestion.

I wondered if I was making another compromise that I should not make. When would Eddie read without prompting? He was old enough to pursue his interests, but those interests never transferred to reading. I knew he wouldn't read a book that he didn't have to read; maybe this would be a way to get him reading about a subject he seemed interested in. Maybe.

On my next meeting with Eddie, we drove to Verona Park and, sitting on a bench facing the water, we started to read about Anne Frank. I cleared my voice and began to read from this beautiful young girl's diary... "On Friday, June 12, I woke up at six o'clock..."

WAVE CAP

"You ever wear a wave cap or a do-rag, Mr. Cooperman?"

"No, Eddie, I never have. In fact, I have never seen any white person, other than an occasional athlete, wear a do-rag or a wave cap. Have you?"

"I haven't either. But I just wondered what you'd look like in one," he said.

With that, he pulled something out of his pocket and asked if I would like to try it on.

"Sure, I will. But first I'd like to know what I'm trying on. Is this a do-rag or a wave cap? I don't know the difference."

"A do-rag is almost always black, and it's not fancy at all. A wave cap is a lot fancier, and it costs about $2. If you put it on your head, it keeps your hair down and makes waves in your hair," said Eddie. "That's why it's called a wave cap."

I told him I didn't need to keep my hair down, but agreed to try on the wave cap.

Eddie adjusted the material and made the various loops and knots with the strings so that the wave cap was firmly in place. He told me it didn't look too bad, but then he couldn't contain his laughter and almost doubled up as he looked at me in the wave cap. I checked myself in the mirror. Certainly, I was a sight to behold, and I started laughing too.

"I don't think I look bad in a wave cap Eddie; it just takes some getting used to."

"Oh, that's good, Mr. Cooperman. I thought I'd try it and see if you liked it."

"Oh, I like it all right."

"You really don't look that bad, but you do look a little funny."

I wonder why Eddie chose to have me try on a wave cap? I was always trying to get him to try new things; maybe he was trying to get me to try something new. Probably not, probably simply a sign of friendship.

A TALK WITH PAULETTE

"So, how is it going with Eddie?" Paulette asked, as I had just come home from my weekly meeting.

"It went great. We played catch with a football and ran imaginary plays against a defense. Sometimes I would be the quarterback, Eddie would be the end, and then we would reverse it. He's getting to throw the football a lot better, and I'll admit it, it was fun for me to throw a football around in October!"

Paulette looked serious and said to me, "I know you're having a lot of fun, but it seems that you don't do much reading any more, and you know Eddie isn't a good student. I just wonder whether you're buying in to his agenda rather than Eddie accepting yours."

Wait a minute – I'm the one investing the time; but ...she's making a good point. Maybe I'm not seeing the forest for the trees.

"You might be right, Paulie," I said. "I guess I am doing too many things that he wants to do. I hadn't really thought about it a lot."

"I know how much you want to prepare him for life, and to help him develop the skills he will need to take care of himself in the world. And, I'm just wondering whether it's going to work out like you wish. Frankly, I'm kind of worried about it," she said.

"You know I wasn't really successful in getting Eddie to read and increase his comprehension and vocabulary. I could sense that he was throwing a wall up between us. To persist might have ended the relationship, and I just didn't want to give up."

"I understand that," she said. "But are you just becoming a friend who goes out with him every week and has fun – fun being what he wants to do?"

"I understand what you're saying. I know he likes me; he respects me; he trusts me. He talks to me about a lot of things that he prefaces with 'now, this is a secret, just between us'. And, when he says that, he knows I will keep it secret and listen to him and give him advice, if that's what he wants. I think I've become not only a friend, but a respected role model. Isn't that worth something?"

"It is, and I'm not diminishing what you have accomplished. But, Eddie is going to be fourteen next week, and his grades haven't improved very much. I'm sure that means he's probably falling further behind in his reading."

"You're right. I guess in the beginning I was thinking that perhaps he might be able to attend a four-year college; I have pretty much given up that hope. I can't ram what I think is right down his throat. If I had Eddie twenty-four hours a day, I could care for him and work with him as I did with Suzanne, Debbie, and David. We had the kids for twenty-four hours a day, and if we said no TV from Monday to Friday, we could make it stick. We could establish an atmosphere that education was important, and keep reinforcing it. That's almost impossible for me to do with Eddie.

"Then are you giving up on the academics and just trying to be a friend and a counselor?" she inquired.

"No, not on your life. We still do some things that are academic. For example, Eddie must always add the bill when we're at a restaurant. He knows this and sometimes he actually looks forward to doing it. It's practical, and he understands that he doesn't want to be cheated."

"By the way, did I tell you of the discussions we've had about Anne Frank?"

"I don't remember you telling me about that," Paulette said.

"Oh, I may have forgotten." I mentioned the conversation with Eddie about Hitler and the Nazis and my ordering the book. I told her that we read and discussed about thirty pages during our two previous meetings.

"Sounds pretty good," she said.

"I'm cautiously optimistic. He seems interested because he wants to know about how the story will end, and what will happen to Anne and her family."

"That sounds good, maybe you can get at the academics this way. But I'm still not really convinced because usually when you come home you say that you played basketball, or tossed a football, or took a walk somewhere, and it sounds like you're doing what Eddie wants. I think it's a situation where he's not looking at you as someone who can help him achieve an end, the way a kid who goes out for a football team looks at the coach. Do you understand what I'm saying?" she asked.

"I do and you could be right. I just know that it doesn't work when I give him a pep talk about the importance of reading and math as a means to an end. Nor does it seem to work when I talk with competent African Americans we meet in restaurants and ask them how they got their jobs. Although Eddie seems impressed by the unrehearsed, consistent comments of strangers, such as, 'you've got to study hard, young man; you've got to learn reading and math if you want a job like the one I have', it still hasn't sunk in enough for him to change his attitude towards school work."

"So, I'm going at it in a way that's a lot different than I intended; whether it will work or not, I don't know. But I'm not abandoning my attempts at making Eddie a better student."

I think I'll continue to be a friend to Eddie first. We do have fun together and this has led to him placing trust in me. The more trust I build, the more, hopefully, he will listen to my advice. While I couldn't be firm with him and challenge him when he was nine, I *can* do that now. He talks *with* me and responds when I tell him "who are you trying to kid, Eddie?"

So, perhaps I am making progress, although not as much as I would like. Then again, I may be rationalizing my progress as a trusted friend for my lack of progress in the academic areas.

I hate to admit it, but Paulette may be right.

SAGGING

"Do you ever sag, Mr. Cooperman?" Eddie asked.

"No, I don't Eddie."

Sagging is the wearing of trousers so far down on your hips that if someone is walking behind a person who sags, they see the "saggers" boxer shorts and might see the beginning of the crack in a person's behind.

I was told by someone I know who works in the juvenile detention center in Newark, that male inmates in prisons are not allowed to wear belts, and many wear their loose fitting pants low on their hips. Because so many of the prisoners are from urban areas, this became a style to be copied by young men in our cities. I don't know if this is true or not, but I do know that "sagging" is very apparent in Eddie's neighborhood, and, in fact, in the entire city.

Because his city and his neighborhood was the only one Eddie knew, and indeed, he didn't stray far from it, he just made the logical assumption that I might also sag. When I told him I didn't, he asked if I sagged when I was younger. When I told him that nobody sagged when I was a kid, he seemed rather surprised. This was just one of many situations that Eddie and I faced, when he was somewhat unbelieving that I didn't do something which was very much standard operating procedure for him.

I told Eddie I wore white buck shoes and blue suede shoes when I was a teenager. He found this hilarious, given that I seem so "straight" now. But, after his laughter he understood that kids of every generation had their fads.

I had made up my mind that there were many things in Eddie's world which I didn't particularly like, but I wasn't going to challenge them because there were other things that were more important. I had to choose my battles. Whether he sagged or not was, I felt, a passing fad. And, even if sagging should last, I don't think he would get far with that behavior when it came time for him to hold a job.

Showing up when you said you would, keeping every promise you make, learning to read and do math well; these are the battles that I deem to be important, and on these I'm not going to retreat.

But will I succeed?

I'M PASSING

Eddie had just received his report card and gave it to me under the watchful gaze of Celie. "It's the same old thing, Mr. Cooperman. I don't know what I'm going to do with him."

I looked at the report card and it was pretty much as she said, an F in math, a D in reading, a D in science, a C in social studies, a C in Spanish, and a B in physical education.

"The B in physical education is good, Eddie, and the two C's in Spanish and social studies show you are capable of doing average work. But, I'm disappointed with the two D's and the F," I said, "very disappointed."

"Well, I'm passing everything, Mr. Cooperman, even with the F in math. That's the first F, and I got one C and one D in math, so I'll pass for the year for sure," he said.

I could feel myself getting more upset and I was annoyed that my emotions were getting the best of me. I told Eddie that passing wasn't the only thing. I told him he could pass and still not be able to do the math. I reminded him about the improper fractions we worked on last week and the trouble he was having. I knew I was probably taking a cheap shot when I said if the teacher gave him a test tomorrow, he wouldn't be able to pass it. I knew Eddie still had difficulty with all aspects of math and often used his fingers to count something that shouldn't be done by an eighth grader.

Eddie didn't help lessen my anxiety when he repeated, "I'm passing, Mr. Cooperman, I'm passing. I don't see the problem."

I couldn't hold back. "That's just the problem, Eddie. You don't see that there's any problem. How many times have we talked about good grades mean a good job? You want a car, but a car costs money. You won't make enough money for a car if you're flipping hamburgers at McDonald's!"

"My friends tell me that if you get A's and B's, you're trying to act white," he said.

That really did it! "Your friends don't get A's or B's so they put down getting good grades. Your friends were the type of people who see everything in racial terms and whatever whites do is no good."

"Eddie, sooner or later, I hope you begin to think for yourself and don't always listen to what your friends say. If acting white means being smart, then perhaps you should think about acting white. Your friends make it seem like it's a bad thing. Well, they're the ones who are stupid. If white kids were scoring twenty-five points in a basketball game, would you want to score five points because you wouldn't want to act white?" Dr. Martin Luther King Jr. and General Colin Powell had to make good grades in order to become educated and later become leaders in our country. Should they not have studied and worked hard because that would have been acting white?"

He was silent.

I was not.

"If you want to own a house like mine, you have to study in order to get a good job and make money and you are not going to get a job unless you know how to read and do math. It really is as simple as that. Reading is the key to everything. If you know how to read, you learn how to think, and if you learn how to think you are able to make good decisions. If you can't read, the chances are that you'll have a job like that guy we saw in the supermarket the other day, pushing a big cart and loading things on the shelf; a dead-end job, and dead-end jobs don't pay very much." I knew I had said this 100 times already to Eddie. But I was frustrated.

Where was the key? How would I be able to reach him? Celie means well and tells him that he's got to do better and if he doesn't, she won't let him outside to play. But I know this won't last much longer because he has begun to challenge her verbally and her threatening does not do much good. For that matter, neither have my lectures.

Passing is important because Eddie wants to stay with his peers and continue on to the next grade. But learning and achieving are not on his agenda. In fact, if he could make A's and B's, this would be negative, not positive. If he learns and does well, he'll be ostracized by his peer group, who, like Eddie, makes C's, D's, and F's.

Everything's backwards! Just like the word "bad," which really means "good" in Eddie's environment. I wish I could take Eddie and put him in a situation where kids don't sag, and where they don't see people being shot. I wish he lived in a neighborhood where male role models come home after a day of work and reinforce the message of persistence, determination, hard work and learning. I wish. But, Eddie lives where he lives, and 'passing' is all that seems to count.

I am at a loss about how to reach him.

Where is the key?

THE BIG APPLE

When Eddie was ten, I had taken him to New York City. It was his first visit to New York, and he was awed by the hustle and bustle. Like any first time tourist, he craned his neck to look at the tall buildings and was somewhat upset by the large crowds that jostled him as we walked from block to block.

We had taken a train and Eddie was excited about going under the river. Even so, he was concerned that the water might come in and the "sharks will get us". My explanation of how tunnels are built and how sharks didn't swim in the Hudson River were only mildly assuring, and Eddie was only happy when the train reached the 33rd Street Station in New York, and we climbed the steps to sunlight.

We had visited the Museum of Natural History and looked primarily at the dinosaurs. He took lots of pictures and was quite concerned that there still could be dinosaurs alive in the United States. On the way home, he said, "Mr. Cooperman, when are we going back to New York City? I really liked that place."

I told him that it probably would not be for a while. Not one to be put off, he would often ask me if we were ever going to go back to New York. I finally relented, and in September of 2002, we planned to spend a whole Saturday in the city.

This time, we drove over the George Washington Bridge, and Eddie was fascinated with the views up and down the Hudson River. He showed no fear of the height and was impressed, as most people are, with the New York skyline.

We first went to the Central Park Zoo, and he was delighted with the antics of the seals and otters. He said he had been to a zoo some time ago, but he was little and really didn't remember it. We spent over an hour and a half at the zoo and saw almost every exhibit.

We left the park and watched some street acrobats performing in Central Park. Fifteen people, ranging in age from about six to mid-twenties, did a variety of leaps, spins, and turns to an appreciative audience of almost a hundred.

"Did you see that guy spin on the pavement, Mr. Cooperman? That looked impossible. I don't understand how he did it."

"He obviously has done a lot of stretching and moving his body around in order to be able to do that. Neither one of us could do it I'm sure."

"He must practice that a lot to be able to twist and turn like he does."

This was my opening, and I took it. "Anyone who's good at anything has to practice it a lot. Remember when we went to the play at the Performing Arts Center? Those singers and dancers had to practice day after day after day to be able to get their dance steps right and be able to sing so well. Both the singers and the dancers had to practice to make sure they had their timing right. Just like an 'alley-oop' play in basketball; it takes practice."

Eddie understood what I was saying and nodded in agreement. "It's the same thing with reading," I said. "You don't get to be a good reader unless you practice. You know you told me that you're still working on your cross-over dribble. I know you're doing that because the last time we played, you were so much better than you were a few months ago."

"I know," said Eddie. "I practice as much as I can. I'm going to beat you with that move."

"You probably will. And it just shows what practice will do. Now, if I could only get you to practice your reading as much as you practice your cross-over dribble, we would be getting somewhere."

Eddie listened thoughtfully, but then decided to change the subject. "Mr. Cooperman, what type of animal would you want to be if you could be any animal?" I knew from many prior situations that when Eddie changed topics, it would be nearly impossible to move back to the prior one. I would be talking to tin ears. So, I played along with the switch.

"Why, I think I would want to be a hippopotamus," I said.

"A hippopotamus! Why would you want to be a hippopotamus?" Eddie asked.

"Well, first of all, I like the water, and hippopotamuses spend a lot of time in the water. Also, they don't have to go far for food. They simply open their mouths in the stream and take in the food that they need. Also, most animals in the jungle have to fear for their lives. And, although hippopotamuses look funny, they are quite strong and nobody really messes with them."

"But don't the alligators go after them?" he asked.

"Not really. They're much too big for the alligators. And, so, they are left alone. Who would you like to be?" I asked.

"I think I'd like to be a lion. They seem to be very fierce, and I don't know that anyone would want to take them on," Eddie said.

After the discussion on "who would you want to be," we walked through several stores. Eddie was particularly impressed with Tiffany's, especially the prices. He couldn't imagine that a necklace really cost $32,500, rather than the $325 he thought was the marked price. "I see what it says, but it's hard to believe that anyone would pay that money for just a necklace," he remarked.

"Well, it seems crazy to me too. But that's because we don't have a tremendous amount of money. I guess if we had a million dollars and really loved someone, maybe we would spend $32,500."

On the way home, as we were nearing Eddie's house, he said to me, after a period of silence, "Would you help me with my math?" Our work in this subject, using the book Suzanne gave us, had started well, but, after two months, tailed off, and then stopped.

Here we go again, I thought. Start and stop, now another start... maybe.

"Ok, Eddie," I said. "But are you just saying that because we had a good time and you think you ought to say something that would please me?"

Immediately after I said this, I felt badly because here he was, again, saying he wanted my help, and I immediately questioned his motives. I couldn't take it back, though I sure wanted to.

"Oh, no, Mr. Cooperman. I really would like you to help me. I think I understand the math, but then when the test comes, I seem to always get D's or F's."

"Okay," I said. "The next time we get together, you bring your textbook and we'll go over some of the stuff you don't understand. But, you have to bring the textbook. I'm not going to keep bugging you. Is that a deal?"

I wonder what it was that made him ask for help. I didn't think it important to know; the important thing was that he asked. But, he has asked before, and he had little commitment. Down deep, what I really think is that he wants me to feel good now, but he has little intention of following through. I'm sad I feel this way, but it is the truth.

So many starts and then stops. This is probably just another of Eddie's good intentions – long on words, short on action.

Too many disappointments.

MATH?

The next time we met, Eddie said nothing about math. I was discouraged but not surprised. But, a week later he said, "Are we going to do math today, Mr. Cooperman?"

Wonderful! Very calmly I said, "Sure, Eddie, let's go to the West Orange Library. We can be in a place where we can work and talk quietly."

The job was overwhelming. He was passed from grade to grade with the most minimum of skills. At fourteen, I estimated he was probably at the fifth grade level. Everything was like pulling rusty nails; he was sloppy in his thinking and writing. He had little understanding of fractions, for example, and converting fractions into percentages and decimals seemed new to him.

During the next few months we worked on math almost every one of our weekly meetings for about fifteen minutes. Progress was very, very slow, but progress was being made. I sure hope it continues.

ANNE FRANK, MARTIN LUTHER KING AND MALCOLM X

We went to the West Orange library on Mount Pleasant Avenue and found a small table in a quiet corner of the library. Eddie asked me if I would read from *The Diary of Anne Frank* first and I was glad to do so. We had been reading a few pages in most of our meetings, and I always brought my paperback copy with me. After I had read a page or two, Eddie picked up the next two entries. And we continued that way for approximately ten pages.

Eddie kept asking why the German wanted to kill the Jews. The idea of mass murder of children and old people was too much for him to handle. He kept asking me, "How could they do that? Why did they do that?" I only wished he were older and could read *Hitler's Willing Executioners* by Daniel Goldhagen. Then he would have a better answer.

I tried my best to talk about anti-Semitism, its religious roots and how it had continued for centuries in Germany. Anne Frank had written about the prohibitions and indignities Jewish people faced, such as being banned from regular school, only allowed to shop on certain days and at certain hours, not able to hold particular jobs, inability to use public transportation, etc.

This was getting to be too much for Eddie to comprehend, but it struck home when I said, "Did you know that black people couldn't eat at restaurants, had to use 'colored' water fountains, and were prevented from voting in the South?"

He said he understood some of this and told me that he knew "all about Martin Luther King and what he did for people." I told him how much I admired King and had recently read a book about his life. I told him how young Martin Luther King was when he started organizing people to help blacks get their civil rights in our country.

He then jumped from Martin Luther King to Malcolm X and asked me my opinion of Malcolm. I told him that while Martin Luther King was a man of peace and believed in peaceful protests, Malcolm X believed that King was going about things the wrong way. He believed that most whites would never give black people equality and if one was threatened in any way, they had to fight back physically as well as with other means. As I attempted to trace Malcolm's life from street hustler to a thoughtful individual who worked hard for his people, Eddie was, for one of the first times, listening to every word I said. I discussed the uneasy relationship between Martin Luther King and Malcolm X and finally Malcolm X's separation from his mentor, Elijah Muhammad.

We must have talked for an hour, with my sketching the main points of the lives of Martin Luther King, Malcolm X, and the times they lived in. Eddie frequently interrupted to ask me why something happened or why something did not happen. I couldn't resist mentioning to Eddie that perhaps he would like to read and learn more about Martin Luther King and Malcolm X.

"I would like to do that, Mr. Cooperman," he said, "but first, we've got to finish the book about Anne Frank."

For my benefit, or did he mean it?

We left the library, drove up Mount Pleasant Avenue and across Prospect to Eagle Rock Avenue and the Chinese restaurant. While Eddie was munching on an egg roll, we went back to the subject we had just discussed. "Do you think that

Martin Luther King and Malcolm X would have become friends if they had both lived?" he asked.

Obviously Eddie was upset with his knowledge that both of these leaders were killed by assassins' bullets. He wondered if they could have come together and used their power to further good.

I told him that I thought it might have happened since Malcolm X had changed quite a bit since he had taken his pilgrimage to the Muslim holy places. I told him I thought Malcolm X had come to appreciate the progress Martin Luther King was making, even if he wouldn't have used King's approach. "I would like to think, Eddie, that if they had lived another ten years, they would have come closer together, maybe not friends, but at least people who could work together for a common purpose. I would like to think that."

This was the first serious and lengthy conversation we have had. Usually our conversations lasted for a few minutes on one topic and then we were off on something else.

Days like this give me some hope.

WAVE CAP II

In early November, Eddie told me that he was going to get me a wave cap for my birthday. (Eddie is fifteen now and I am going to be sixty-eight, well into the Medicare generation.) We had talked about wave caps before and, as I mentioned, I had told Eddie that I didn't think I ever saw anyone who was white, outside of sports, wearing a wave cap. I also thought I'd look sort of silly with a wave cap on since I usually wore a suit to work.

"Well, you don't have to wear it to work," Eddie said. "You can wear it when you're home or when you're working outside in your garden. You know it's really good for your hair. It'll give you waves."

I said that I thought it was good of him to think about me, and I would wear it. I sure didn't want to discourage him, and he was being so caring, wanting to do something for me.

I was further amazed when he said, "Your birthday's December 18, isn't it?"

"You're right, Eddie. How did you know that?"

He told me we were once discussing birthdays, and he asked me when was my birthday and Paulette's. He remembered what I told him. I thought to myself, how sweet that a fifteen-year-old kid would remember my birthday when I'd mentioned it only once. I was touched. I also thought that if he remembered that, perhaps other messages were getting through. My children had resisted certain things my wife and I believed in, only to make these attitudes and behaviors their own in their late twenties. The situations were different, I knew, but I hoped that some things were beginning to rub off.

I had seen Eddie on December 16. We had a good time, read a few more pages of *The Diary of Anne Frank*, and after eating a burger, talked about Eddie's plan to try out for his high school's ninth grade basketball team. He hadn't tried out for his middle school team, and he knew the odds were against his making the freshman team. Eddie said try-outs would be occurring soon. I didn't want to discourage him, so I asked him a few questions and encouraged him to make sure he was present the day try-outs began.

On Friday, December 24, I met Eddie again and brought some Christmas presents for him, one for his brother Duane and a large tin of cookies for the family. As I was getting out of my car, shopping bag in hand, Eddie came bounding down the steps with a big smile on his face, and handed me a small gift-wrapped present. "I meant to give you this last week, but I forgot and I'm sorry. Happy Birthday and Happy Hanukkah," he said.

Hanukkah was long past, but I sure appreciated his remembering and was touched by the two "happy's".

Eddie told me I could open it on the sidewalk, but since I had already felt the package and saw that it was soft, I thought to myself, could this be a wave cap? I suggested to Eddie that we go into his home and I could take the presents out of my shopping bag. After I did this and he put my presents in a corner of the living room, he excitedly returned to his present. "I hope you like the color, Mr. Cooperman. I think you will," he said. Now I knew it was a wave cap!

I opened his package and there it was – a purple wave cap. I moved the strings around the front of my head and secured it in the back, without being helped. I was an old pro at putting on wave caps. I got the same response from Eddie that I got the first time, hysterical laughter. "Do I look that bad?" I asked.

"Oh, no. In fact, you look great," said Eddie, the budding diplomat.

"Well, if I look so great," I said, "then why are you laughing?"

"It's just that you don't see many white people in wave caps," he said, "but you look good, really."

I kept the wave cap on while we took a ride in my car but told Eddie I was not going to wear it when we got out of the car. He understood.

While driving Eddie home later that afternoon, I pulled to the side of the road and put on the wave cap. Eddie was impressed. "Are you going to wear it home?" he asked. "Yes, I am. I want to surprise Mrs. Cooperman."

Later, when I was almost home, I stopped for a red light and a woman in a car beside mine glanced over at me. Our eyes met for a moment and she looked at me with an expression somewhere between amusement and fear. I smiled and she abruptly looked away.

I drove home to be greeted by Paulette with more laughter. I kept a straight face and said, "Actually, I think I look pretty good in this." Paulette and I have never really agreed on the way I dress, and so she just shook her head, smiled and walked away.

I'm happy with my wave cap and didn't give a hoot about how I looked.

A WALK IN THE WOODS

During our last two meetings Eddie had been asking about walking in the woods.

"How come you are so interested in the woods?" I asked. "Whenever I mentioned that subject before, you always told me you didn't want any part of that. So why the change?"

"I was a little kid when I said those things; now I'm more grown up, and I'm not afraid," he said. "I would like to see what's going on in the woods. You are always saying how nice it is, and the animals won't hurt anyone."

"Okay, we'll go next week. Have your mom prepare some lunch for you and plenty to drink. You'll need plenty to drink because we'll be walking quite a bit. I'll bring my own lunch and some veggies for you." That got the predictable "you can't be serious" look I anticipated.

The next week he was ready. His backpack was filled with three sandwiches, a large bottle of water and some napkins. While we were traveling to the Audubon Arboretum, Eddie said, "I'm not really afraid, but will there be any snakes where we are going?"

I said that the snakes usually sun themselves on the rocks, and, since it was about 45 degrees and overcast, I didn't think we would be seeing any snakes. I thought this was correct, from my Boy Scout days, but I really wasn't sure. Eddie trusted my word.

We began our walk on the Loop Trail and left the path when we came to the stream. I was pointing out various birds and trees and Eddie's response to my enthusiasm was a consistent, "uh huh." I thought to myself, "This is going to be a short hike." Then, I pointed out something that I thought might bring forth at least some interest since my children usually spent a minute or two looking and listening to my comments.

"Do you see this tree trunk on the ground, Eddie?" He nodded. "Well, at one time this must have been a beautiful tree; now it is in the process of decaying, and going back into the earth." I pointed to the lichens on the bark, and small insects of various sorts working on the wood.

Eddie was fascinated! Never had any of my children showed so much interest in this particular area. The questions tumbled out of his mouth. "Does that little spider eat the wood? Do the ants and the spiders ever fight each other? What do you mean that the dying tree provides for a new tree? Why does one tree live and the other one die? How can a little tree have a chance if the big tree has so many roots? How will a little tree get any water, the big tree roots will get it all, won't they? Why do the woodpeckers only make holes in trees that are sick or dying? Why does that vine wrap around the tree? How can the tree live when it is being squeezed like that?"

I never had so many questions so fast. I tried my best to answer as many as I could.

Perhaps I should have stayed in the Boy Scouts longer, I thought.

We must have spent a half-hour by the decaying trunk of the one tree. And we moved at a glacial pace as Eddie discovered one dead branch after another. He wanted to know why one tree that was obviously dead was still standing and why some larger trees were on the ground with their massive roots exposed. Discussions of wind, rain, and erosion followed and then it was time for lunch. We talked only of the woods and what was going on in this quiet place; no basketball! After lunch we decided to walk more and see if we could climb a "mountain." For a novice, he caught on quickly. He was careful with the wet leaves and rocks and climbed well. He was careful not to break any branches and was pointing things out to me the way anyone would who was having a good experience. When we arrived at the Audubon Center we had walked about four miles, not bad for a first time hiker.

****

As we were leaving the center, Eddie asked, "Why did you give that man money?" He was referring to the Audubon volunteer who was watching over the exhibits and the various items for sale. I told Eddie that the exhibits and the care of the trails cost money and I wanted to say that we appreciated the four hours we spent in the woods.

"But, the money won't go to the Audubon, that guy will pocket the money," Eddie said, somewhat upset with my naiveté.

"I don't think he will, Eddie. I believe most people are honest and this man is a volunteer so he gets no salary. The money isn't important to him or he would get a job that pays him a salary."

This led to a conversation of Paulette's work with hospice, and why people volunteer. With money concerns always a constant in Eddie's life, he was still struggling to understand who volunteered and why. He knows that I volunteer my time to be with him, but why large groups of other people volunteer is something that is still difficult for him to grasp. Especially when they could be making money!

Eddie paused and then launched into one of his most consistent "what if" conversations. "What if we cut down a tree, would the cops arrest us?"

I asked if he thought people would cut down a tree and he said, "Probably not."

But, he didn't back off, "If someone did, would the cops put him in jail?"

"Not if the police didn't have any problems with him before. He would probably be fined and put on some sort of probation."

"What about the shirts in the room next to where that volunteer guy worked?" Eddie asked.

"What about them?" I responded.

"If you stole one of them, would you go to jail?"

This frequent asking my advice on the chances of getting caught and the consequences had gone far enough. This wasn't the first time Eddie had asked questions about theft, apprehension, and punishment. Every time he had previously brought up the "what if" scenario before today, I would answer his question, but, not today.

"Eddie, if you are thinking of taking something that isn't yours, I hope you get those thoughts out of your mind. I know you see kids who steal and get away with it. If they steal and don't get caught, they will make stealing a habit, and sooner or later they will get caught. They will have a police record, and that will make it hard for them to get a job, or get a loan to buy a car or a house," I told Eddie. "I know you won't admit it, but I'm concerned you are thinking about stealing, and that's why you are asking so many questions when we are together."

On one hand, I knew by saying this I would force Eddie into denial, and he might not want to bring up subjects he thought I might disapprove of. That would negate any influence I might have in this area. But, on the other hand, I wanted him to know, in no uncertain terms, what I felt and why. I wanted him to know that there were "rights" and "wrongs" and there were things that people should and should not do.

"I wasn't thinking about stealing, Mr. Cooperman," he said with righteous indignation. "I wouldn't do anything like that."

"I can't look inside your head, Eddie, but this isn't the first time you have asked about the penalty of taking something that isn't yours. When a person has a continuous interest in something, it means it's on his mind," I said. "You have told me many times that I am your friend, and I am proud that you consider me your friend, but, friends must talk honestly with each other, even if the conversation is difficult. So I'm saying that stealing is wrong; if it's not yours, then you keep your hands off of it. If you weren't thinking about stealing, then I'm sorry for coming on so strong. But, this is important to me, and you must know how I feel."

He again said that he just wondered what the penalties were for certain crimes, and that didn't mean he was contemplating anything. I had one more salvo to get across and said to him, "You will start to make more and more decisions by yourself, rather than have your mom make them for you. And as you make these decisions, you will be determining the type of man you will become."

"I wouldn't do anything like that, Mr. Cooperman, I was just asking, that's all."

To me, that wasn't all. His environment was exacting a toll, a powerful pull on him. Some of the kids he knew had juvenile records, and the drug dealers were very much in business. I was more than concerned, and I hoped my confronting Eddie meant he probably would stay away from these "what if" type of questions about stealing. I resolved to talk about right and wrong and not back off. I want Eddie to know exactly how I feel about things, and that I would work my values into our conversations.

The stakes are getting higher. The "dark side" certainly has its appeal. We were having such a great time; now I feel like I've been hit in the gut.

GOD IS GREEN

We had visited the Sacred Heart Church in Newark. I wanted Eddie to see the beautiful building, but, of more importance, the sanctity of the house of prayer.

After we left the church, I asked Eddie, "Did you see the people praying in the church?"

"Sure I did," he replied.

"Do you ever pray, Eddie?"

"All the time, but I can't tell you what I say."

"I just wondered if you prayed, that's all."

"Do you pray, Mr. Cooperman?"

"Yes, mostly for people who are sick."

"Did you ever pray for yourself?"

"I did once. I had just learned that I was going to have a very big job, and I hoped I was up to it. I asked God to allow me to work hard and to make good decisions."

"I think God is green, Mr. Cooperman."

I was startled at the statement and change of direction, but I recovered and said, "Why do you think that?"

"Well, it seems that black people and white people fight a lot, so God couldn't be either white or black. That wouldn't be fair. So, I think he must be another color, like green."

From the mouths of kids.

SKIN DEEP

Eddie and I were reading *The Diary of Anne Frank* in Verona Park.

He looked at me after reading a passage and said, "Why isn't everybody made the same?"

"What do you mean by that," I asked, "I don't understand."

"The Nazis killed Anne Frank because she was Jewish, and white people killed black people because they look different. So if we all looked the same, maybe people wouldn't kill each other. If God loves us, why didn't he make us all the same so there would be less killing?"

Whoa! I didn't know what to say. I stumbled for a few seconds and admitted I didn't know why God did what he did. "Animals are different, and so are insects," I said. "Maybe God just made a lot of different things to see if we could somehow exist together."

This didn't sound right, and my mind was racing. I thought about animals that kill other animals, but they usually do this only for their existence, for food. I thought about territory and turf and how man and other animals are similar in this regard. But the thoughts weren't coming in a coherent fashion and I said simply, "I don't know why, but we are different and the idea is to respect our differences and not let things like religion and skin color get in our way."

We talked more about why people hate and I emphasized my belief in Martin Luther King's words "Judge me by the content of my character, not by the color of my skin". This conversation went on for about an hour; a new record.

Then Eddie said abruptly, "Are we going to the Chinese restaurant today?" I had promised him a return to the restaurant so we packed our book and water bottles and were off.

Sadly, our experience in the restaurant was an extension of our conversation about Anne Frank, the Nazis and God. Our waiter handed us the menus without comment and took our order without saying one word. I thought he might just be out of sorts, but this was not the case. On five separate occasions I had to look for him to request water, chopsticks, tea, a spoon, and fortune cookies. Never did he say a word to either of us.

Eddie noticed his behavior and asked, "Why doesn't he ask if there is anything we need; we have to look around and then ask him for things."

I wasn't completely honest with what I was feeling, "He might be upset about something; maybe he doesn't feel well, or perhaps someone in his family is sick, so he isn't attentive to us." While this may, indeed, have been true, I hadn't had such a poor waiter in many years. Was I over reacting or was the reason for the waiters neglectful, bordering on surly attitude, the color of Eddie's skin and my association with him?

I was very upset and left a five percent tip so the waiter would know I hadn't forgotten the gratuity. Rather than confront him directly and get a predictable denial, I decided to talk with the manager of the establishment; I gave her the facts about the waiter's inattentive and rude attitude and left it at that. I thought if I stated what I felt, she might think I was overly sensitive and transferring my dissatisfaction with the service to an unwarranted conclusion. So, I stayed with the facts, let her see Eddie and me together and let her draw her own conclusions.

That lousy waiter. I despised his attitude. Maybe I wimped out and should have confronted him anyway.

THE FIRST JOB

Last week, with the permission of the manager of the local McDonald's, we stepped into a large walk-in cooler. Eddie wondered where they kept all the hamburgers, rolls, French fries and other foods. When I told him that restaurants had very large refrigerators and freezers, he said he wanted to see one.

"Who takes care of the food in case the refrigerator breaks down? Our refrigerator broke last year and all the food spoiled; we had to throw a lot of stuff in the garbage," Eddie said.

"People who learn how to fix refrigerators do, Eddie; they are mechanics with special training."

I told Eddie how my uncle Bill owned a refrigeration business in East Orange, and that I worked for him one summer. "I learned how to cut copper tubing, put rubber belts on motors, and help bring the right tools to my uncle. It was very hard work."

"Did you want to be a refrigerator repairman?" asked Eddie.

"No, I didn't really like taking motors apart, like my uncle Bill did in his workshop. So I knew that type of work wasn't for me," I said. "But, he made a good living doing that work; he bought a house, cars, and sent his son to college."

I asked Eddie how much he thought a refrigerator repairman made today, and he said "twenty dollars an hour."

"Well, Eddie, if you multiply that by three, you will be closer to the right number."

"You mean he makes $60 an hour and the guy cooking hamburgers only makes $5 an hour? That doesn't seem fair."

"Maybe not, because they both work hard, but shouldn't a man who studies and learns more be paid for what he knows? Not many people can do what the refrigeration guy can do; so, if they want him to fix what is wrong, they have to pay him for what he knows."

****

I had been hammering Eddie with education/work/money linkages for several years now. Although I was making progress in many areas, this was not one of them. Perhaps if Eddie had a real job, some of this would sink in.

I had known Harry Richardson for ten years. Harry runs a day care center in Newark, and is a keep your promises type of guy who was sincerely interested in helping Newark's children. I thought Harry might give Eddie a job in the day care center, and I asked him if this was possible. Harry said it might be, but he wanted to see him first.

"I want to meet the kid," said Harry, "talk to him and see if he really wants to work."

I agreed to bring Eddie to see Harry the following week, and immediately began to worry about Eddie's possible behavior. He could sometimes posture that he was a tough and confident kid, but he was basically shy and tended to avoid people he didn't know.

The week before the meeting with Harry, I met with Eddie twice and we held interviews. "Keep your head up, Eddie, and look at me and don't mumble ... Why do you want to work this summer? ...Are you going to show up on time? ...How will you get to the day care center? ...What are you going to do with the money you make?" Eddie understood that this was important and did a good job of answering my barrage of questions, with no wise remarks.

"I think you are ready," I said, "now what are you going to wear?" Again Eddie surprised me when he said, "I think just a shirt and pants, no chains or wave cap, but, I can sag, can't I?"

I knew he was teasing me and I said, "Sure, I'm certain Mr. Richardson will be impressed that you sag."

The big day finally arrived and Eddie was silent as I drove him to the meeting. I tried talking about basketball, which was always sure to start a spirited exchange, but not today. My worry quotient was soaring and I could just see Eddie freezing up and Harry saying, "I'll have to think about it, Saul; I'll give you a call."

My concerns were unwarranted and Eddie breezed through the interview. I was proud that he handled himself with poise which I hadn't seen before. Then Harry asked, "What do you think I should do if you come in late and then don't show up at all and give me some dumb excuse?"

"I don't know," said Eddie, and he shot a look of desperation in my direction.

Harry turned to me and asked me what I would do. I said, "I would tell him he is through, the job is over."

"That's exactly what I would do," said Harry. "But, let's not talk about stuff like that anymore; I think you will do just fine and I'm offering you a job starting July fifth at $5.50 an hour. Be here at ten in the morning and you'll work until three in the afternoon. Do you have any questions?"

"No," Eddie stammered, "but thanks, Mr. Richardson, I'll be a good worker."

On the way home Eddie was on top of the world. His math skills didn't allow him to figure out in his head how much he would make each week, or for the whole summer. Since he was beside himself wanting to find out how much he would make, we pulled to the side of the road near Sacred Heart Cathedral and I gave Eddie a pencil and paper. He multiplied five hours times $5.50 and determined he would make $27.50 each day. With five days in a week he would be rich! After the euphoria of learning how much money he would make each week, I broke the news to him about taxes and social security. He didn't like that at all but seemed resigned to the fact that he couldn't do anything about it.

I also reminded Eddie that we had made a deal that if he got the job he would take one out of every five dollars and put it in the bank to save for a big purchase. Eddie "sort of" remembered the conversation then became excited when he picked his big purchase to be a Playstation 2. I estimated that Eddie would net almost $1000 if he worked every weekday until Labor Day. With Playstations costing just over $200, Eddie might get his Playstation by the end of the summer.

Before Eddie got out of the car he asked me why I said he should be fired if he came in late or was absent without a good excuse. "Because you have been using that stomach ache excuse for years and I wanted you to know how I still feel about it. I just wanted to make sure you wouldn't try that with Mr. Richardson. Sooner or later, you have to learn that if you try to con some people they will do things you don't like. I thought you would get the message and I have to tell you that I was pleased Mr. Richardson felt the same way."

Eddie smiled, thanked me for helping him get the job, and got out of the car.

I called Eddie three times during his first week of work and everything seemed to be going well. Eddie was on the janitorial crew and his job was cleaning the lunchroom, playrooms, hallways and bathroom. I had told him to do every job as if I were going to inspect it, and do it better than his boss expected it to be done.

"I've been doing that, Mr. Cooperman, but my boss keeps telling me to work slower and that I don't have to clean behind the toilet like you showed me."

"Keep doing what you are doing. Some workers do as little as they can and don't want anyone else to 'show them up.' These are the goof-offs of the world, Eddie, and you should learn not to be like them. Continue to do the very best you can do; it will pay off in the long run. Always do more than expected. If your boss continues to tell you to slow down, we'll talk about it when I see you in a few days." Luckily, he didn't, and Eddie continued to clean behind the toilets.

One day after Eddie was on the job for three weeks Harry told him that he noticed Eddie swabbing down the kitchen area when he only had to sweep it clean. Eddie was excited when he told me that Harry said, "That's the way to go, Eddie. Good job." Two weeks later Eddie was removed from the janitorial gang and was assigned to be a teacher's assistant, working with three year olds. "I like working with kids," said Eddie. "I know what to do because I've had experience with my cousins. Mr. Cooperman, I was wondering, do you think Mr. Richardson had something to do with my getting this job?" Eddie asked.

"I think so," I said, "after all, he saw you mopping the floor and he probably knew everyone else just swept it. Mr.

Richardson is successful because he works hard and he respects hard workers." I believed what I said, but more importantly Eddie believed it, and saw for the first time that his working hard and doing something extra paid off.

Eddie worked for almost eight weeks, took two buses to work every day, was never late, and never missed a day of work. I was proud of him and told him so. We celebrated after his last day on the job with a pizza and some ice cream. I ate a turkey sub and was on top of the world.

PLAYSTATION 2

We had opened an account at the local bank, and for the first two weeks, Eddie had conscientiously put in 20 percent of his earnings. When it was time to put in his third and fourth weeks, Eddie only had $10 to deposit. "What did you do with the money," I asked.

"I bought some school clothes for myself and I gave my mother $50 to pay a bill." I thought about his answer for a minute and told him I was going to ask his mom about the clothes, but not about the $50.

Eddie just shrugged his shoulders and said, "Don't you trust me?"

I felt bad but I anticipated his question. "This is the first time you have ever had a large amount of money and we made a deal that you aren't keeping. I guess I feel I have to check this one out."

I asked Celie if Eddie bought some new clothes with some of his earnings and she said, "He kept pestering me about two Tommy Hilfiger shirts that cost $60 each and a jacket, and I told him I wasn't going to buy it for him; he had money and could use that if he wanted to." I gently reminded her that we had agreed that if Eddie got the job he would put in 20 percent of his earnings every week. "Yes, I know that, but he really wanted the clothes for school, and I didn't want to pay for it because he really didn't need that stuff."

Again, I found myself in a situation where I would alienate Celie if I kept dwelling on the promise. Though I might win the battle, I could lose some future wars. So I backed off.

Unfortunately, this became a pattern and Eddie only had $105 saved by Labor Day. No Playstation 2. During the next two months Eddie would often ask if he could take the money out to spend on one thing or another. I told him that was not possible; he had to honor his word. "I know a deal is a deal," he fed my words back to me.

"Right, Eddie, and I'm going to see to it that you keep your end. You didn't put enough in and you are not going to take it out. You don't like what I'm doing now, but we must both sign to get the money out and I'm not signing." My friend was not pleased.

And, two weeks before Christmas, when I called to just shoot the breeze, he gave me the ultimate guilt trip, "Mr. Cooperman, I always have to ask my mom for a few dollars to buy Duane, my cousins, and my mom Christmas presents. Couldn't I just have $50 to spend on them so I don't have to ask?"

I took a deep breath and said, "Eddie, I'm sorry that you didn't think of this sooner; I know you are only fifteen and some things aren't going to occur to you, but I'm trying to teach you something about money. Remember when you were younger and you asked me how I got a car, a house, and other stuff? It's no different than your Playstation 2. You have to make up your mind that something in the future is more important than spending everything you have the minute you get it. When you get the Playstation 2, you will see what I mean. So, no, I won't sign for the $50."

There was silence on the other end of the phone and then Eddie said, "I don't think you are fair."

Oh, well…

BYPASS

Things happened fast. I felt something funny in my chest. Not any of the signs of a heart attack, just different. Paulette and I went to the hospital for what I thought would be a "nothing to worry about, but let us know if anything else occurs" kind of comment. Even though I had an angiogram a few years ago and had some blockage, somehow I didn't think that this was anything serious.

What I got was, "We're admitting you and I've scheduled an angiogram for tomorrow." Later the next day I got the news; four of my arteries were over 90 percent blocked and a coronary bypass was necessary; the sooner the better. I knew this was always a possibility, especially since my mom and dad had died of heart attacks.

I had tried to avoid this situation by eating right, exercising, and not smoking. Unfortunately, heredity seemed like it was trumping my efforts.

The surgery was successful and I was home in three days. I had canceled my weekly meeting with Eddie and called him to let him know what had gone on. I decided to keep things simple and said, "Eddie, as you know I've had a problem with my arteries; that's why I eat all of those vegetables and don't eat hamburgers and fries. Well, I had to have an operation last week."

"You're not going to die, are you?" he interrupted. "You'll be okay won't you?" Obviously, my understating the problem hadn't been successful. "Do you have to have other operations? I asked a teacher about why you eat what you do and so I know a lot about arteries." So, my little man had been checking up on me! I was really touched.

"I'll be fine, Eddie, but I can't play basketball until the summer. I just have to take it easy for a while." I tried changing the subject, "How are you doing with your girlfriend." Eddie had taken a girl to a dance, his first, and I had been asking him about her since that time. I called her "his girlfriend" to tease him and get his usual, "She's not a girlfriend, I just kind of like her a little". It didn't work this time.

He brushed off my question and returned to, "You sure you're not going to die?"

I feel really good," I said, "in fact, Mrs. Cooperman will be driving me to see you next week. If I were going to die, do you think the doctor would let me drive to see you?"

"No, I guess he wouldn't, but why can't you drive?"

I explained that my chest was a little sore and he accepted that without comment. Our conversation drifted to some usual subjects, math, basketball, and the appetite of his brother, Duane. "Duane would eat anything; you know that awful stuff, that Moo Shu Chicken you eat at the Chinese restaurant, well, when I took some of that stuff home, he ate it in a few bites. I never saw anything that he didn't eat."

He is important in my life. I always knew I was important in his. I just heard confirmation again.

RETIREMENT

Paulette and I decided that it was time to smell the roses. She had a bout with cancer six years ago, and the bypass operation got my attention. Although we are optimistic about our health, we are also pragmatic about what could happen.

And work, though interesting and challenging at times, after ten years was becoming somewhat repetitive. My boss was a great guy and cared deeply for people who were struggling to keep their families together. I felt badly about leaving him and his work, but the usual enthusiasm I normally brought to any job didn't always seem to be there.

Our conclusion was that I would leave my job, and look forward to greater independence and control of our time. We resolved to visit family and friends more, travel often, vacation in Florida in the winter, and pursue individual interests.

I thought about the effect this would have on Eddie. He was fifteen in October. Spending three months in Florida in the winter would test our relationship. I would write and call, of course, but nothing replaces face-to-face meetings. On the other hand, I would see him more often and for longer periods of time the other nine months. Mostly, I've been seeing Eddie after work during the week. Although I did see him on an occasional Saturday or Sunday, this was an exception as I reserved weekends for family. Now, I would be able to see him for greater lengths of time during his vacation periods, and much more frequently on the weekends.

We bought a condo in Florida and I wrote to Eddie. Generally, I would write twice before I would get a reply. His letters were informative about school, his family and playmates.

On the phone he was more expansive, telling me how hard he was working in school and how the next marking period was going to be better. He didn't seem at all upset and took the long separation in stride. He seemed to adjust too well, and I called him one evening and said, "Eddie, are you worried that I'm in Florida? Do you think I'm pulling away from you?"

He laughed and said, "I'm not worried; you're my friend and I know you're not leaving. I understand."

I would like to think that is exactly how he feels. I hope that being there for him and keeping every promise I made has given me his trust, confidence, and respect. Too many people have disappointed him. I hope our eight years together have proven to him that I really care.

Because I do.

Eddie

Ages 16 to 21

CELIE

I like Celie very much. She is probably in her early forties and I have seen her now for almost eight years. Although her material possessions are few, her apartment is always clean, an oasis among neighborhoods that are in decay. In the three times she, Eddie, and Duane have moved, there are always goldfish swimming in a tank, and decorations on her apartment door for the major holidays.

But, the thing I admire is Celie's positive attitude. She is always smiling and is optimistic about the future.

"How is life treating you, Celie?" I might ask.

"Just great. The job is interesting and I enjoy what I am doing."

"How is your mom these days?"

"She is good although she sometimes forgets things and repeats a lot. But, we see her every week."

"Does she still work with Meals on Wheels?" I asked.

"No, she stopped doing that a few months ago. It became a little too much for her. She is doing well, though, and said she looks forward to our getting together again."

Celie was a stay at home mother for the first few years I knew her, subsisting on various welfare programs. There was not a negative stigma to welfare in Celie's neighborhood, and the word "welfare" was not used. "Public Assistance" was something the government provided, much like other government programs. It was just something a person received if their circumstances warranted it.

When the welfare laws changed, Celie was required to seek employment. This presented a major problem, since Eddie and Duane were young and making sure they were safe was her primary concern.

Celie had to get a job near home, to enable her to be there if a problem arose with her boys. She did not finish high school, which further complicated the situation. But, with her usual "can do" approach to everything, she landed a job at the Great Kids Learning Center. Initially, she answered the phone and filed papers. But, her supervisors saw her ability to take charge of a situation and get things done, and gave her additional responsibilities as a teacher's aide.

Celie walks to work every day, a distance of almost two miles and has been with Great Kids for almost six years. Her children see Celie as someone who goes to work every day and, by doing this, is a constant positive example to her children. Eddie and Duane, like most kids, watch what adults do, rather than what they say. Celie's deeds match her words.

Before I started the mentoring program in Newark in 1993, I met with many people who headed Big Brothers and Big Sisters mentoring programs at the national and local levels, and read books and articles on the subject. One aspect of dealing with parents was that a mentor might be asked for money to pay a bill, or help the family out of an emergency. Often, this "asking" would be constant and the mentor could become a source of financial help. Everyone said this should not be done and giving, if at all, should be confined to birthdays, Christmas, and perhaps some other special occasions.

As I got to know Celie, I saw that this might be easier to say than to do. There was so much that was needed and I wondered how I would react if asked.

I was never asked. Celie is such a prideful and independent person, that she would rather do without, than ask for help. Once I bought a large fan to be used in the summertime, and I have taken the family out for lunch on several occasions. At Christmas, I have bought large tins of cookies for everyone, but that is about it. Thank goodness I have not had to say "no" to Celie, because I have never been asked.

When Paulette was ill, Celie sent a card and frequently inquired as to her health. I just hope that Eddie will ultimately get a good job and help take care of his mom the way she has taken care of him and Duane. In neighborhoods that beckon with rotten choices, Celie has seen to it that Eddie and Duane have done what is right and resisted the temptations of "the street". Meeting and seeing Celie all these years has given me an appreciation of what one person of character can do when pitted against neighborhoods of warped values.

EDDIE'S FUTURE

It's the winter of 2002-2003, and I've been Eddie's mentor for more than eight years. He has grown from a little boy who held my hand when we crossed the street to a young man of sixteen who notices girls and whose voice is deepening. In two years, he will graduate from high school. (I hope.) The high school graduation test looms over the horizon and math is still Eddie's Achilles' heel. He is doing better in math but now he doesn't have me there every week to help him from January through March. He says he is using the self-help book I gave him.

Celie continues to be a positive influence, often stressing that it is important to finish high school. I've heard her say many times, "If you want to get a good job, you've got to finish high school. I didn't, and now it's hard for me to get my GED."

I've followed Celie's lead by tying the high school diploma and a good job together. Eddie wants some of the material things most of us want. He likes my car and wants one of his own. He wants a home of his own where "a landlord can't turn off the heat or not fix the front door".

Eddie tells me how hard he is working out doing push-ups. This, of course, gives me the opening to talk about developing his mind as well as his body. I frequently talk about the material things he wants and tell him what it takes "upstairs" to get a car or own a home.

I try to keep it simple, repeating what I've said before. "Banks won't loan money to anyone for a home unless they feel that the person has a good job, and experience leads them to believe the person they lend money to will pay them back. If a person works on and off and is not dependable, they won't give a loan to them. If anyone has a criminal record, they probably will deny a loan because they will feel the individual is not trustworthy. Just like in school, where you get a report card, in life, you get report cards, too."

He has finally made the connection between hard work and money and wants to return to the day care center again this summer. From my conversation with Harry Richardson, that will be no problem because of his performance last year. But, the link between school work and a better job than the day care center hasn't been forged. I will keep trying to help Eddie make that connection.

So, where am I now? I think he is a young man of good character; he has avoided the gangs, has no juvenile record, understands right from wrong, and has a charitable heart. I wish he belonged to a church to hear beautiful messages of love and kindness, but Celie does not think that is important. We talk about being a good person and what that means, and I am very satisfied that he has good values and strong character.

As I've mentioned, he understands what it is to work. He has seen me at work, and he knows that good work will have monetary rewards. We haven't progressed to talking about work that is fulfilling or work as a means of making society a little better. That type of talk wouldn't work. But, the bank account and the Playstation 2, though not successful so far, has reinforced my basic point: if you work hard and well, have a goal and save, you can get what you want. I think I am getting through to him in this arena, even if it is a major struggle at times.

Understanding that education has value, and that a trade or skill is important still gets token acknowledgment. I'm baffled that I haven't made more headway here but I haven't. His mom is a perfect example of a hardworking woman with few skills. She puts in a lot of good effort but doesn't command a high wage. He sees his father as a man who does not work. He gets angry with people who won't work and he won't give a penny to people with their hand out and tells me not to do it. But, he has not internalized that the McDonald's manager, the accountant, and the refrigerator repairman all have skills that they have attained through study and training and they make more money because of it.

Right now, the more than one hundred dollars a week he makes at the day care center seems like a fortune to Eddie. So, why does he need to study and get good grades? He's worried about math because the teachers have put the fear of God into him that half of his tenth grade classmates will drop out before graduation.

I think in the next year or two he will want to make more money and set his financial goals higher. When his "wants" require thousands of dollars, he may see the practical necessity of learning a skill. Education will be seen as a means to an end of getting more money. This is not the way I would like him to think in this area, but it is the way I think it will play out. For example, he wants the Playstation, but hasn't saved enough money to get it. And, I will not buy it for him. Not for his birthday; not for Christmas.

We have more than two years until Eddie graduates. I intend to be at his side every one of those years. I want to see him with a skill that will enable him to be valued by employers. I know he will be a person they can trust and depend upon. He will not be able to give me courtside tickets to the pro basketball team he thought he would play on, but I will be only too happy to let him buy me a meal at a restaurant. I will enjoy that, especially if he checks the bill before he pays it.

I've heard Elger's "Pomp and Circumstance" at many graduations. I will be proud to hear it at Eddie's.

FEEL MY MUSCLE

Eddie is maturing. I see the wispy hair on his upper lip and his elbow is no longer the widest part of his arm.

"I do push-ups every day, Mr. Cooperman. I want to look like Michael Jordan."

"Do you run much, Eddie?" I asked. "If you want to look like Michael Jordan, you have to run and run."

"I don't run at all, except when I play basketball. What do you mean 'do I run'?" he asked. I tried to explain the difference between aerobic exercise and building muscles, and Eddie listened intently. "I agree with what you say. MJ has to be tough the way he gets hammered and then he has to run to get back on defense. He is a great defensive player. He made the all-pro defensive team so he can play both ends of the court. How much do you think I have to run, Mr. Cooperman?"

The words came out in torrents. If only he would show the same enthusiasm for reading and math! "I think if you could run around the block in less than three minutes that would be okay for now. It's about a quarter of a mile. Maybe in a week or two you could do a half mile in less than six minutes. Then, we'll go from there."

"I read in one of those sport books you gave me that a football player said he got strong just by doing push-ups, sit-ups, and pull-ups. Is that true? Was he telling the truth?"

"I think you may be talking about Herschel Walker who said he never lifted weights. He might have gotten results that way, but most people get stronger by lifting weights. Your birthday is coming up soon. Would you like to have some weights for your birthday, Eddie?"

A few weeks later, I wished Eddie a happy sixteenth birthday and gave him two 5, 10, 15 and 20 pound weights, together with a booklet on exercises with the weights. Eddie promised to lift every other day and wouldn't go past the 10 pound weights until he showed me he could do three sets of ten repetitions on each of the exercises.

Within two months Eddie was running a mile in under eleven minutes and working with the fifteen pound weights.

"Feel my muscle, Mr. Cooperman. I'm getting much stronger; I know I am."

I dutifully squeezed his right and left arms and agreed with him.

If this would be his approach to academics also, we would be near the goal line.

MATH – THE ACHILLES HEEL

We worked at math. Fractions into decimals, decimals into percentages, long division, simple geometry and word problems. It was frustrating to me and to Eddie.

On one hand, he had to improve in order to pass the high school graduation test. On the other, he approached the task as if it were the last thing he wanted to do. This made for meetings filled with an undercurrent of tension. I would try to praise him when he seemed to really understand something, but he knew his progress was minimal. Too much praise and I was a phony, not enough and he was ready to quit.

The underlying gut issue was that Eddie just didn't see why it was so important for him to learn math. At times I would get tired of giving examples that I thought should have made sense to him. For example, we went into a supermarket where I had been hours before, and asked him if the super sized detergent was a better bargain than the smaller size.

"Of course it is. The larger the size, the lower the price," said Eddie, right on cue.

"You are probably right, Eddie, but how can we know for sure?"

"I don't know; I just assume the bigger size will be the better price."

"Do you have your calculator with you?" I asked.

"Ha, ha….you think I keep it with me all the time?" he joked.

"Okay, let's do it the long way. If we know the ounces, we can divide the ounces into the price and find out how much each ounce costs."

"Are you really going to do this, Mr. Cooperman?" Eddie asked.

"No, you are. I like to save as much money shopping as I can. Don't you?" I said.

"I guess so, but this box says two pounds and ten ounces. I forgot how many ounces are in a pound."

"There are sixteen ounces in a pound, so how many ounces are in this package, Eddie?"

He quickly gave me the correct answer, forty-two ounces. I just happened to have a small piece of paper in my pocket and a pen, so the rest was easy for Eddie, dividing the ounces into the total cost. When we did this for the smaller box, Eddie was amazed to see that the smaller box was actually cheaper.

"Why did they do that, Mr. Cooperman?" Eddie asked.

"Maybe a lot of people think as you did, Eddie, and most of the time the larger item is the cheaper one. But not always. That's why it pays to check." (I did not point out that this was already done, as the cost per ounce was posted on the shelf. Since Eddie seldom shopped, I was devious in getting him to figure out the relative cost of the larger and smaller detergents.)

Once we went to a Macy's store when they were having a storewide sale. I also had a coupon that gave me an extra ten percent off any price. I really needed some t-shirts and we looked at the selection. The regular price was indicated and I asked Eddie to do the math; the fifteen percent storewide reduction on this item, plus my coupon for the additional ten percent.

Everything I could think of became a math problem. Sometimes Eddie would groan, but he dutifully tried to solve the practical situation I put before him.

"Most people are honest, Eddie, but some will cheat you if they see you don't know math. They will take advantage of what you don't know. You should want to keep every cent that is rightfully yours in your pocket, and not have someone take your money when they don't deserve it."

I knew when to stop, but sometimes I got carried away, and my lecturing turned Eddie off.

The nub of the situation was this – Eddie thought he would somehow be able to pass the graduation test. That was all he cared about ...passing. Learning and integrating the knowledge was not on his radar screen. So, we were fundamentally working at cross purposes.

Our agendas met in our study sessions as Eddie slowly learned some more math. He could now do the multiplication tables in his head and the long division was becoming second nature. When he got a "C" on his next report card, he was pleased, and then began missing some of our sessions.

I acted childlike when I canceled a session when I didn't have to, because of his casual attitude. Then it was back to the distance and time problems, and the next week, some practical problems involving a rock star, with ticket sales, shirt sales, percentage to rent the facilities and the agent's fee.

Sometimes the practical nature of the problems I devised appeared to get his interest more than the book examples, but the tension between us was there. Why, I asked myself, was I doing this when he really doesn't seem to care? Maybe I should just let him fail the damn test and then see what his reaction will be.

But, I didn't do that with my children when they didn't seem to understand so I had to keep plugging away with Eddie.

CHERRY LANE

My dad was always walking with me in the woods across from our home in West Orange. The "cow pastures" were gently rolling hills where cows probably did graze at one time. Dad and I walked and talked, and generally ended our hike by skipping rocks or sitting by the bank of Vincent's Pond. My uncle Bill also took me on walks. We would go to Cherry Lane, in nearby South Orange. It was a large county park with some open areas, big rock outcroppings, and streams. Uncle Bill was happy to climb, walk and just sit and talk with me. He showed me the various trees and talked with me about nature. I owe to my dad and my uncle that I loved biology in high school and college, and still enjoy the beauty and quiet of the woods today. How lucky to have such men in my life.

Now it was my turn to try to interest Eddie in something other than the city streets. At first Eddie saw no purpose in coming to Cherry Lane, even though we had taken several walks in the woods near my home in Bernardsville. He didn't fear the woods anymore, but that didn't mean he liked them either. But, I had the car and Eddie loved to talk so he made the compromise.

We would usually walk around and then pick out a place to sit or lie down on a reasonably flat rock. The conversation would range from the trivial such as, "The Nets will never win unless Jason Kidd shoots more. If he does, it will open the inside to easy baskets," to "If there is a God, then why are innocent people shot by gang members? Why isn't God looking out for them?"

I felt good that Eddie felt comfortable with me and every conceivable subject was "on the table." And, because his questions were better and had more depth, he was beginning to realize that I didn't know everything and that I might not, "clean up on Jeopardy".

Our relationship is good. I look forward to seeing Eddie and his beautiful smile each week. When I arrive, he usually tells me how much he enjoys our time together.

Things are going well.

ALL IS WELL

Eddie and I spent the day in Bernardsville. We played some basketball in the driveway, but Eddie's passion for the game has waned. Without much discussion on the topic, I felt Eddie understood that he wasn't pro material.

When Paulette called us for lunch, Eddie was eager to sit down, because he knew what was on the menu: macaroni and cheese, chicken, and orange juice.

"Thanks, Mrs. Cooperman, I really like the way you make the macaroni and cheese." Paulette did make it from scratch, and I think Eddie liked it because she loaded it with cheese.

After we had finished with lunch, Paulette asked Eddie how he was doing in school. "Everything is good, Mrs. Cooperman, although I am still having trouble with math. I just don't seem to be able to do all of the problems."

We decided to walk to downtown Bernardsville, about a twenty minute stretch of the legs. We visited Marx's "Department Store" which is reached by entering a realtor's office and taking a stairway to a basement. There, the sole proprietor, Mr. Marx, was waiting; ready to talk with anyone who made the trip downstairs.

In a sense, his establishment was a department store, since it had a wide variety of items for sale, everything from fabrics to irons, Boy Scout equipment, shirts, shoes, watches, and overcoats. But, the real feature was Mr. Marx, who seemed ageless, and greeted everyone with a genuine smile and a ready story.

"What is your name, young man?" Mr. Marx asked.

"Eddie," my friend responded.

"Well, Eddie, where do you go to school?"

Eddie hesitated for a few seconds and then said, "Cecily Tyson High School."

"Isn't she an actress, or a singer?" Mr. Marx asked.

"She is both, and the school has emphasis on the performing arts," Eddie said.

"Are you going to be an actor, young man? Can you sing?"

"Oh, no, I just go there because the school isn't as big as East Orange High School and my mother thought it would be better for me."

"Who knows, maybe you will learn to perform on the stage, and be a big star," Mr. Marx quipped.

"I doubt it," said Eddie, "I can't sing very well so there isn't much hope for that."

After a few minutes of talk, I asked Mr. Marx to show us around the store, something he was most willing to do. He showed Eddie various items and told us that he would order almost anything that people wanted. I asked him how he could stay in business when the malls had so many stores with a tremendous assortment of products.

"I guess they like to come to a place that will try hard to have what they like, and everyone in town knows that I will take anything back if people are not satisfied."

After we left Marx's Department Store Eddie wanted to talk about Mr. Marx. "He seemed like a very nice man. He seemed to be interested in where I went to school and what I was doing. I can see why people like him and shop there."

"You are right, Eddie. Getting a product for the lowest price is usually important, but some people will pay a little more for the personal attention they get from Mr. Marx."

We headed back to our home and spent the afternoon sitting on the deck and talking. I can't remember much of the conversation, except that I felt good about our relationship and Eddie's relaxed manner with me.

All is well, I thought………………… I thought wrong.

THE HSPT SURPRISE

On the High School Proficiency Test (HSPT), New Jersey's standardized graduation test, a student must make a passing score in reading, writing, and math to be awarded a diploma. If a student fails the test in the eleventh grade, he still has three more chances to pass the test in order to receive his diploma.

I am continuing to work with Eddie in all his school subjects. But, I only see him once a week and I work with him on schoolwork for fifteen to twenty minutes each time we meet. And, in January, February, and March I am in Florida; while we speak on the phone and write to each other, there is no "tutoring."

I thought Eddie had a good chance to pass the reading, as his comprehension was acceptable, and he reasoned well. However, writing was another situation. He would read a few pages of a story I selected and then I would ask him to respond to a few questions in writing.

His word usage was not good, to say the least. Patterns of speech, reinforced over time, had become part of his writing. I found myself saying over and over, "Could you have said it this way, Eddie?" He would understand in that moment, but habits were hard to break. I thought of all the conversations we had about the environment and keeping public and private spaces free of litter; when Eddie was with me he was a true "picker upper", but I remember his throwing the McDonald's container into the street that one day before he walked to his home.

I tried to use his success at running and weight lifting to make my point. "You are running a mile in ten minutes, Eddie, and lifting twenty pounds with each hand. You've come a long way in a relatively short time. You did this because you worked hard, day after day, week after week. You are an inch taller – Eddie is now 5'7" – and you are five pounds lighter so you are doing lots of things right and seeing the results. Now you have to make the same commitment to your mind."

"I understand what you are saying, Mr. Cooperman, I really do," he said.

How many times have I heard that, I thought.

We worked through the fall, and through December. I bought Eddie a self paced book that focused on reading and math. Answers were in the back of the book. "Okay, Eddie, now you are on your own. I don't watch you run or lift, and now I can't be with you for the next three months. How much you work and learn is your decision."

In the spring, when Paulette and I returned from Florida, Eddie had not received his scores on the HSPT. "Did you get the HSPT results, Eddie?" I asked.

"No, not yet, maybe next week," he replied.

The next week and the week after that came without the results.

"Maybe they are slow in coming, Mr. Cooperman."

"Something is wrong, Eddie; maybe they lost your results; it can happen. If it's okay with you, I'll get a letter from your mom allowing me to meet with the principal and guidance counselor. I'll ask your mom when I see her later."

"Mr. Cooperman, I have something to tell you…" There was a long pause and then Eddie continued, "I haven't been going to school since October. I've been meaning to tell you."

I was hurt and angry. I couldn't believe what he was telling me. He had dropped out of school!! "Your job was to get a diploma. You say you realize how important that is, but really, you don't care. What the hell do you think you are going to do?"

"I'll get a job."

"That means you don't have a job. What have you been doing the past five months?"

"I've been at home, watching TV mostly. I feel badly about what I did because I know I let myself down and I let you down. But the teachers are terrible; they don't care about the kids at all."

Eddie planned to ask Mr. Richardson for a full-time job. I told him if he got a full-time job it would be a crummy job at low pay. "You have no skills, Eddie, and you have to have something to offer an employer." I was having a difficult time controlling myself. I had failed Eddie, and Eddie had failed himself.

"So, you are not planning to go back to high school next year?" I asked.

"No, that is a rotten place. I'll get my GED, you'll see. I went to a place and know what I have to do to pass it."

"And for the past five months you haven't done anything but watch TV. I'm taking you home, Eddie, I've had enough."

I told Paulette I would not see Eddie for a long time, if ever. All that I had tried to do, all the talks, all the role models, all the tutoring, down the drain. I had hit rock bottom.

No more; I've had enough.

MUCH WORSE THAN ROCK BOTTOM

Paulette seldom complains, and when she was concerned that the stomach pain hadn't gone away after two days, I was more than concerned.

Preliminary tests indicated some blood imbalance that could be serious, but other tests tended to be normal. Blood tests and several "procedures" went on through April and May without a specific diagnosis. Then, toward the end of May came the dreaded words, "pancreatic cancer".

I called everyone I knew who could possibly help; surely there had to be a way to beat this disease. I finally settled on Dr. John Chabot, who practiced at Columbia Presbyterian Hospital in New York. Dr. Chabot gave us hope and said that new combinations of radiation, chemotherapy, and surgery could give patients a chance at an almost normal life. If Paulette responded to the chemo, and, if Dr. Chabot could get at the cancer and get it out, then Paulette would be able to eat most foods, go on vacations, and do most of the things she wanted to do.

Paulette was beyond strong. She suffered through the radiation, the chemotherapy and pain killers, through the hair loss and weight loss. For most of the time, from June through December, she insisted on cooking and doing what she normally did, albeit at half the speed. She was a rock.

And, we talked about Eddie. I had not seen Eddie in five months. He had written to me three times telling me how sorry he was, how he had learned from dropping out, and that he was studying for the GED. I did not respond to any of his letters.

"Saul," said Paulette, "he's only a kid; he did a stupid thing. Many of his friends drop out, you know the statistics. In his neighborhood, leaving school has no negative stigma. Give him a chance."

"You were the one who said he was playing me for a sucker. You were right. He got what he wanted from me, and in the most important thing I wanted from him, he blew me off."

"He loves you, I can see that; he wasn't doing this to hurt you, he just made a big mistake. Give him a chance," she said. "Don't personalize it, Saul."

When Paulette wanted something in our marriage, she usually got it. I jokingly called it the "Paulette Water Torture"; she would come at the same subject many different ways, with many tactics, always persistent and always with the same objective.

"Okay, I'll see him," I said after a month of conversation and water torture. Around New Year's we met, and somehow he sounded different; more mature and more focused. I wasn't sure if I just wanted to believe him, but he seemed sincere and determined.

"I'm working half time for Mr. Richardson, but the job isn't a good one. I work two hours in maintenance, cleaning, and the other two hours helping teachers with the pre-school kids." He went on, "I understand that if I don't get the GED I probably won't ever get a good job and make good money. So, I bought a book about studying to pass the GED and I'm going to take it in the spring." He showed me a savings account and he was depositing $20 every paycheck.

At least he's doing something right. Maybe he was serious, but maybe it was the same old bull; when it came to doing physical stuff, he was ready to pay the price, but, studying? I wanted to believe, but a big part of me was wary, very wary.

I told Eddie about Paulette and tears welled in his eyes. He always smiled and was eager to see Mrs. Cooperman. "Will she be all right? She's not going to die, is she?" I told him I thought she would be okay, but this was a very difficult disease.

In January, Paulette told me she wanted to go to Florida. "Why not, Dr. Adler said I was done with the chemo and I have to wait a month and gain some strength before the operation; I want to go and be in our place." And so we went, and had a pretty good time, under the circumstances.

When we returned, Dr. Chabot said the cancer had "retreated" but Paulette was still not a candidate for surgery. "You have to have more chemo, Paulette; I'm sorry, but this round should do it." She took a deep breath and said, "Okay, I've come this far, I guess I can survive some more."

She did, and on February 24, 2004 at five in the morning we headed for the hospital. For the first time since May she said, "I'm scared." I did my best to reassure her that we had to believe Dr. Chabot and that she was going to survive and thrive. Dear friends of ours had previously let us use their vacation home in Jumby Bay, Antigua, and Paulette thought it was the most beautiful and peaceful place she had ever seen. I told her that when she was ready, the first place we were going to was Jumby Bay. I told her what we were going to do when we got to Jumby Bay and how we were going to ride our bicycles, eat the wonderful food, and take quiet walks in the moonlight.

Paulette endured three operations over the next three days, totaling twenty-two hours. Dr. Chabot said getting the cancer out was the easy part. Reconnecting the arteries after the surgery was very difficult because Paulette had been a cigarette smoker and her arteries showed the wear that comes with smoking.

"She is so strong, Saul," said Dr. Chabot. "She has come so far. I think she will be okay."

I want to believe. I have to believe.

THE ULTIMATE LOSS

Dr. Chabot said, "We have to keep her sedated for about ten days, to let her body heal from the operations. She has been through a lot." On March 6, Paulette opened her eyes and said simply, "Hi Saul." She then asked what time it was and I said 3:00 PM, but it was twelve days after her first operation. Ever feisty, she told me, "If you think that's funny, it's not." While I was happy to see her spunk, I had difficulty convincing her as to what had happened and what she had endured.

She spent a week in the intensive care unit, and then two days in the "step up" section before being transferred to a private room on March 17. And all through the next two weeks John Chabot was there, caring and compassionate. One day he stopped in and told Paulette he was going to write about her case in a medical journal. I felt great because he used words like "remarkable" and "wonderful recovery".

Unfortunately, as good as Dr. Chabot was, the rest of the hospital staff was uneven, and that gives them the benefit of a lot of situations. Nurses told me they had so much paperwork to do they couldn't give more attention to the patients they served. Several times I had to demand that nurses come into Paulette's room to perform necessary functions that I knew needed to be done. I made sure that a member of our immediate family was always with Paulette during the day and a practical nurse with her every evening. There were mistakes and neglect by the staff every day. I wanted family or a trained professional with her every minute.

And she got better. During the end of the first week in her private room she announced to me that she had walked to the door of her room, about fifteen feet, earlier that morning before visiting hours began. By the end of the next week she had walked about twenty yards to a solarium, and she was justifiably proud. Although she was less than 100 pounds, Dr. Chabot said she would be going home in less than a week. All I could think of was how I was going to get her back to 135 pounds.

From February 25 to March 30, Paulette improved day by day, slowly but surely, Dr. Chabot's skill, positive attitude, and her determination made it seem as though our hopes would come true. But a fistula hadn't healed itself, and Dr. Chabot said a minor operation was necessary.

"It is nothing to be concerned about, and she will be back in the room in less than two hours." She was joking as she went into the operating room.

When Dr. Chabot came to see us, his face told us everything. "Paulette is dying. The arterial connections are dissolving and it is impossible to reconnect them. I am so very sorry, but we cannot save her." My love was gone. I could not understand how it was all taken away. Could this be true? Maybe it is just a vivid dream and I will wake up.

It was no dream.

ALONE

I learned to cook, to shop, to clean, and to iron; chores I had never done. If I ever wondered what Paulette did, I knew now, in detail. Oh, yes, and I cried. For someone who hadn't cried since I was a child, this was something I couldn't control. At the sound of a song, a thought that would come into my mind, or waking from a dream, I would cry. A friend of mine had given me a book, *When You Can't Stop Crying*, so I knew others felt as I did.

There were so many reminders, and they seemed to be with me every hour, every day. One time I was driving on Route 80 in New Jersey, going about 70 in a 65 zone. I passed no cars, but many were passing me. Then, I noticed I was slowly overtaking a car, probably the only one observing the speed limit. For some reason I looked at the license plate and thought it said "Paulie." A chill went up my back as I drew closer. Yes, it seemed to say, "Paulie" and an "8" after the name. That made no sense to me, but as I came almost behind the car, I saw it said, "Paulie B", and I started to cry in the car. Her middle name was "Beth."

I know that people grieve differently, and losing a mate is something that happens. But, I had a very hard time coping with the reality that I was alive and Paulette was not. This was not the way it was supposed to be. I was to be the first to go, why did it have to be this way?

I struggled to see my children and grandchildren. My daughters and son had lost their mother yet they were wonderful to me. I spent lots of time with them, holding on to those most dear to me. And my friends were there for me. I understood when some married friends invited me to dinner once or twice, and then silence. They were married and I was now a widower; times had changed. But, thank God, enough people were there to call me, meet for lunch, or send an email.

I realized that no matter how I ached, I had no option, but to go on. The world was not going to grieve with me. And, then there was Pablo.

Pablo Komara called me one day and said, "Let's form an educational company." I had known Pablo in college, but our lives had taken very different paths upon graduation. While I had become an educator, Pablo had entered the world of finance. As I was to find out, he had become very successful, followed my career, and now, in his late sixties, wanted to try something new.

Pablo and I formed a consulting company and I was back in harness, so to speak. I enjoyed the work of a start up, and enjoyed working with Pablo. He was intelligent, with a mind that devoured information. He was fun to talk with and good to work with. He meant what he said, kept his word, and when he said, "Saul, it is your call," he meant it.

So, slowly, I re-entered the world as it was, not as I desperately wanted it to be.

I had only seen Eddie a few times during Paulette's illness. Now, I would give it one more try to see who Eddie was and what he wanted to become. I had no idea if I would be different, less understanding of his struggles, because of my loss and my grief. I would try, but I wasn't sure that I could tolerate any more "slippage" on Eddie's part.

ANOTHER YEAR

It's 2005, Eddie is eighteen. He kept his word about studying for the GED, using the workbook I had given him. And, he paid his fee to take the GED with his money, not mine. After two tries at the GED, Eddie had passed four of the five sections on the test. He had failed math, his nemesis, and to pass the GED, one must pass all five sections. He seems very positive and feels he is just a few word problems away from passing the math section. I'm still wary, but perhaps if I could get him to understand the geometry aspects better, he would get all of them right and that might put him over the top. I decided to offer him some "tough love".

"Take the train to Bernardsville, Eddie. I'll meet you at the train station and we can spend two hours or so working on math." I still wasn't 100 percent sure Eddie wouldn't backslide and I wanted to see just how much he would put into this effort.

"Sounds good to me," he said. "I've got plenty of time on Saturdays; what time would be good for you?" The first two sessions went well. We reviewed fractions, percentages, decimals and then tackled geometry. Then, the old Eddie seemed to reappear. He missed the train one week and "I had to help someone move" the next week.

Here we go again, I thought. Screw it – I am not going to call him. Eddie called me to set up some sessions and, somehow, he righted his ship and there he was, on time and ready to go the next four weeks. I kicked myself a bit, but knew that I was only trying to protect myself against another disappointment. I so wanted to believe that he was fundamentally different now.

And, he seemed to be starting to understand why the angle was 45 degrees, and not just guessing because it looked like it was a 45 degree angle. Eddie went into the exam confident and came out confident. "They asked some of the problems we went over last week. I know I got all of them right."

Three weeks later he called me and said that the test center couldn't find his results. Was this true, or had Eddie cooked up another thin lie to cover his coming up short?

"What are you going to do, Eddie?" I asked.

"I will have to take it again, but the woman said I won't have to pay because it was their fault."

A month later he took the math test again and came out smiling. "They gave another test, but, lucky for me there was more geometry on it. I'm sure I passed it."

During the next two times we met, Eddie was thinking ahead. "When I get the results, do you think I can get a better job with Mr. Richardson?"

"First things first, Eddie. Let's see if you passed." I realized this was somewhat negative and I asked, "What type of work would you like to do? Maybe what you would like to do is something other than what Mr. Richardson can offer you."

There was no mention of basketball. "Maybe I could be a trainer in a gym. I would like that. Or, work in a doctor's office." (Eddie has a girlfriend who is working as a phlebotomist.) "Janine said she loves her job, and it makes her feel good that she is helping people. Or, I think I would like to work in a lawyer's office doing something. Someone told me that realtors make a lot of money; I see lots of 'for sale' signs up so someone is making money. I think I would be good as a salesman."

Obviously Eddie had no shortage of ideas. But, he was not a high school graduate.

A few days later that changed with an excited phone call. "I got it, Mr. Cooperman, I passed the math and I have the certificate in my hand. I'm so happy."

FINALLY!

A PROMOTION

I called Harry Richardson to let him know that Eddie was now a high school graduate. "That's great," he said, "I know he wants a full-time job, but he wasn't going to get it until he passed the GED."

"Well, he passed it. I think he has become a very solid young man, one who is looking for greater responsibility. I hope you will consider an increase in pay since he has proven to be an excellent worker."

"Yes, he has. All reports from his supervisor are positive. What do you think he should be paid?"

I was surprised Harry would ask me that question and I must have stammered a bit. But, then I said, "I think $20,000 would be fair. I feel strongly that he is the type of young person you would want to have in your organization."

"I asked because I trust your judgment, Saul. I think that is reasonable and will meet with him in the next week or two."

It took several weeks before Eddie met with Mr. Richardson. He called me that night and said, "I'll be working full time in two months, and I'll be getting a raise from $7,500 part-time that I make now to $20,000 for a full-time job. If I worked full-time at my current pay that would be $15,000. So, I'm getting a $12,500 raise from my current pay or $5000 raise if I kept the same job, and worked full-time."

Eddie's math was impeccable and I asked him what he would be doing.

"I'll be an administrator, doing all sorts of work around the office." Eddie wasn't specific and I thought "an administrator" might mean office work. But, it was full-time and the raise was excellent.

After Eddie began his work he realized that a lot of it was the classic "gofer" position: copying, filing, errands, handling simple phone requests and so forth. But, his immediate superior saw that Eddie could do certain tasks on the computer and gave him some computer related work.

"I know he is happy with what I can do on the computer, Mr. Cooperman. He had no idea I could do some things. I guess on the other stuff I have to start at the bottom. But, it is a good change not having to do the maintenance work anymore or working with the kids."

Two weeks later Eddie called to say that he had not received any pay raise; he was working full-time but his pay was at the same rate as the part time job, which translated into $15,000 a year.

"It is probably just a mistake. Sometimes the payment people aren't notified. Would you like me to call Mr. Richardson and see what the problem is?"

"No, I'll handle it; I was just so disappointed. Do you think when they correct the error I'll get back pay for working the two weeks?"

"I don't know, Eddie. I assume they will be fair; I've always found Mr. Richardson to do whatever he said he will do. He always keeps his promises."

The next paycheck did make up for the back pay and the salary was adjusted, but only to $17,500. Eddie was pleased with the big pay day but upset because $17,500 was not $20,000.

"We can do several things, Eddie. First, check with payroll to see if they didn't make a mistake. If they didn't, there are several things to consider. I can call Mr. Richardson, you can see him, or you can swallow and accept the $17,500."

Eddie didn't hesitate for long. "I'll see him. He promised me so I have to face him."

A week later Eddie called and was shook up. "He told me all I was going to get was $17,500 and if I didn't like it I could quit."

I could feel the anger inside me. Harry was a tough guy but he was always fair with me, a straight shooter, and a man who kept his word. "I don't get it, Eddie. This doesn't seem like Harry. I would like to call him if you don't mind."

"I know you mean well, Mr. Cooperman, but I think if you did that, he might fire me. I don't like this either, but I need this job. I guess I just have to learn that some people I want to trust might not always tell the truth."

I knew that he had so many adults disappoint him; this was just another situation where an adult said one thing and did another. I just didn't know what to say.

As I was thinking what to say, Eddie said "I'm going to work hard, but I'm also going to start thinking about another job."

"Okay, Eddie. Let's both think about this and talk it over when we meet next week."

I never thought this would happen. Not with Harry. What a kick in the rear!

BUT, ON THE OTHER HAND

Eddie adjusted to the new work, but still was upset at not getting the raise he had been promised. We would go out for lunch and talk about how Celie was doing or his girlfriend, Janine. We didn't talk much about basketball anymore. I told him I was disappointed because my courtside seats just went up in smoke. We both had a good laugh about that one.

Eddie's main concern now was his grandmother. I had met Mrs. Johnson on several occasions and immediately liked her. She was a caring and thoughtful person. Twice I had invited her to join Celie, Duane, Eddie, and me for lunch.

She was gracious and always asked me about my family. She told me what she was doing and how pleased she had been bringing a noonday meal to people. Now, she was entering into the foggy world of dementia, and Eddie was struggling to understand. "Sometimes she is just like always, but other times she asks the same question over and over." We talked about this for some time and it was so evident to me the caring Eddie has for his grandmother.

But, life goes on, and Eddie was now serious enough with Janine that he wanted me to meet her. "You will really like Janine. She is funny and has a great job. Not only that, but she has a car."

A few weeks later, I met Janine. I thought I might have to fake it if I didn't like her. But, Eddie was right, she was wonderful. I talked with Janine about how she got her job and did she like taking blood from people. It was obvious that she saw herself as part of a team who would be helping people attain better health. Janine, I felt, was going to be very good for Eddie.

One afternoon, a month later, Eddie talked about his grandmother and Janine, and then abruptly changed the conversation and asked if I had any ideas on how he might go about getting a better job.

"I don't see any future in working at Mr. Richardson's. The people are nice and all that, but I'm not doing much that is new and I want to continue to learn and better myself. And, I'm still upset about the pay raise."

"What do you think you might want to do, Eddie?" I asked.

"I talked with a realtor and I think that it's a great job selling houses. If you sell a house you get a commission. One guy I know says he made a lot of money in real estate sales. If you pass a test you get a license and then it is all up to you. I think I'd like that."

This monologue by Eddie was followed by, "Maybe I should try to go to college. Bloomfield College is near where I live, and I've heard that I could probably get the tuition paid for by the college."

This wasn't going to be a one hour conversation, and sure enough we talked and talked about each of the possibilities. Like Tevye in *Fiddler on the Roof*, there always seemed to be an argument to be made "on the other hand". Slowly, but surely, Eddie saw that a four year college wasn't a good option. And, trying to get a degree as a part timer meant he probably wouldn't graduate until he was twenty-five or even older.

Eddie was talking more and more about the work he was doing with computers and how much he liked that aspect of his work. I thought this might be something to pursue. But, then, again, it could be his "flavor of the week."

When several weeks went by and his fascination with computers continued, I said, "Eddie, if you get additional computer skills that might be something you would like and also be valuable to an employer. No matter where you work or what you do, knowledge of computers will be something that you can use to sell yourself."

"I'm excited about computers and I think that is the best thing for me, Mr. Cooperman. I'm not sure what I want to do, and I agree that this might make me more valuable to an employer."

A few weeks later Eddie showed me a catalogue of courses from DeVry College. He had one course, particularly, in mind, Computer Forensics.

"I talked with someone at DeVry, and they said there is a great demand for people who have forensic computer skills."

I remember that, years ago, Eddie said he wanted to be a cop when he saw that basketball wasn't going to be his meal ticket. Perhaps this was still somewhere in his mind.

"Do you think you might want to ultimately be a police officer, Eddie?"

"No, but working on crime situations seems like it would be a good thing."

This time, I feel in my gut, that he is for real.

DEVRY OR NOT DEVRY

"That is unbelievable, Eddie. If you go full-time to DeVry you will have everything paid for."

"That's right, Mr. Cooperman. They will pay for my tuition, room and board, books, and even transportation. I can't wait to get started. But, I want to attend DeVry and still work full- time at Mr. Richardson's. I can do it."

Eddie was admitted to DeVry College, formerly DeVry Institute, and is convinced that by developing his computer skills, he will make himself more valuable to a prospective employer. Concurrently, he has decided there is no long term future with Harry Richardson.

"How long will you have to attend DeVry to get your Associate Degree?" I asked. Eddie and I had been talking about continuing his education for some time and he had visited DeVry twice.

"Just about one year if I go three nights a week and take one course online each semester," he said. "I would also take courses during the summer."

So, Eddie enrolled at DeVry and was scheduled to begin classes in February, 2008. I was concerned that his enthusiasm might fade when he had to work at the day care center from 9 to 5, and then take a train to New Brunswick and attend classes from 7:00 PM to 10:00 PM three nights a week.

We met the following week and he couldn't be more enthusiastic. For two hours the conversation was almost entirely about DeVry and where he might get his next full-time job.

"Next time, I'll show you my books and the courses I'll be taking," Eddie said. "I'm going to DeVry next week to discuss what I will have to take in my first semester and then get my books."

When I stopped by Eddie's home two weeks later, he had his books piled on a table in his living room. Beside two computer courses, he had to take an English composition course and a course in mathematics. I understood the first twenty pages of one computer book, and the remaining 150 pages could have been written in Mandarin; I was out of my element. "Eddie, do you think you can handle three evenings a week, and still do your full-time job? These books don't look easy to me."

"Sure, I can do it. I'll do whatever homework I have to do on the weekends."

On one hand I didn't want to discourage Eddie in any way, but I also didn't want him to take on too much and then fail. "I know you are enthusiastic, Eddie, but this is a lot of education. You will be taking a train to get to New Brunswick, and won't get home until after 11:00 PM three nights a week, and then you have to be at work by 9:00 AM. This can get to be a difficult grind."

"I thought of that and I can do it," he said.

I had one more salvo and I said, "Okay, you certainly are determined, and that's great. But, keep in mind you have a full scholarship, a completely free ride; you can always switch and go full-time."

"I know, and the counselor at DeVry said he thought I should go full-time. But, if I did that, I wouldn't have a job and then I wouldn't have any money."

"You could always get a part-time job on the weekend and make over $100. That would give you pocket money and still enable you to contribute to your mom for the upkeep of the house. The prize is the Associate Degree, Eddie, learning and applying what you learn so you can dazzle a prospective employer."

"I agree that getting skills will impress an employer, and that is why I want to go to DeVry. I don't expect to need to go full-time, but that is something I will think about if I can't manage the job and college."

I couldn't believe we were having this conversation. Here was Eddie, the dropout, the kid who rebuffed almost all of my attempts to get him to learn, whether it was homework, word games, pleasure reading, etc. Now, he was telling me how important DeVry was to him, and how he would succeed.

I am so glad I didn't give up on him; I was so close.

Thank you, Paulette.

DAY CARE SETBACK

"They put me back with the kids and in maintenance," Eddie said.

"Who put you back, why did they do this?"

"Mr. Brown, my supervisor. He just said they don't need me in administration. There isn't enough to do."

I was livid. Harry had promised me he would "load him up with responsibility, and see what he could do." Now, without any real explanation he was told to go back to his prior responsibilities.

"Do you want to accept this, Eddie?" I asked.

"If I quit, I would need to get another job. It might take a few weeks and I would lose the salary. I'm really angry, but I think I should just stick it out for a year."

I made the offer to talk to Harry.

"I appreciate your wanting to do that, Mr. Cooperman, but he wasn't nice to me when I mentioned the $20,000 he had promised me. I'm afraid if either you or I spoke to him, I'd get sacked."

"The option to go full-time is always there, Eddie. You might learn more without working a full-time job, and going to school three nights a week. And, that's what counts, what you learn and can apply."

"I want to try it this way. I really feel I can do the school work and do the job."

Eddie is sounding more like an adult. He has considered his options and made a decision. My job now is to support him, which I will do.

"Good for you, Eddie. You really have thought this through like an adult. Just don't ask me for any help on the computer courses."

"Mr. Cooperman, you said you would introduce me to some of your friends who might have a good job for me, or recommend me to someone."

Eddie didn't know the term "networking" but he was doing just that.

"I sure do know some people, Eddie. Let me make a few calls and set some things up."

"That's great. Thanks, Mr. Cooperman."

My man is growing up.

GRAMMAR, PUNCTUATION, AND ALL THAT STUFF

Eddie emailed me an assignment he has at DeVry and asked if I would read what he wrote and make suggestions.

"What is it exactly you want me to do?"

"I have to write 500 words on cell phones and 500 words on junk foods. I have to give my opinions on each and can say whatever I want, as long as it makes some sense."

"So, why do you need me to review it, if it is your opinion?" I said.

"Sometimes I don't exactly say things the way I want to; you could point things like this out to me, and I will try to say it better."

I wasn't going to write Eddie's paper for him, but said I would give him my opinion as to how he made his points.

Eddie's thinking was fine, but his grammar, punctuation, verb usage and such were terrible. Things he should have learned and committed to habit in grade school were not learned. And the sad part was that Eddie did not know what he didn't know.

For example: "There are groups called environmentals", "I think Healthier Foods are", "Brussel sprouts are labeled as disgustingly nasty", "Some organizations are trying to foil the populations of deer's".

When I pointed out a few of the more glaring errors, Eddie said, "I should have known better; I was in a hurry." I mentioned the right way to say things in a few examples, but was not going to give an English lesson over the phone. Eddie was slowly coming to grips with the seriousness of the problem as I explained why his words were not correct.

He would have to work hard on the fundamentals of grammar and punctuation, as well as writing in a more coherent manner. I talked about his errors until I was sure he understood that he needed a lot of work in this area, and he really didn't "know better".

Eddie was carrying a pretty good load with the part- time job and the heavy academic program at DeVry. If he were able to get by at DeVry without his teachers taking him apart on his shortcomings, I was not going to throw more information at him now.

"Eddie, when you learn computer applications, you will have to express yourself in writing. You may know what you mean, but if you can't communicate it clearly to others, you will not advance. Knowing in your head and expressing it in writing are two different things."

"I think I can learn what I have to quickly; will you help me?"

"Sure, I will Eddie; let's see how it goes at DeVry. If they don't land on you for this, then we will work on it this summer, when your schedule is lighter."

"Okay, thanks, Mr. Cooperman."

Better late, than never.

DEVRY AND UPS

"I did it, Mr. Cooperman; I quit my job with Mr. Richardson, and got a job with UPS."

"That took guts, Eddie; what do you do at UPS?" I asked.

"I work from 5:00 PM to 11:00 PM lifting boxes off a belt and putting them in piles for shipping."

I was so proud of Eddie for doing this by himself. He saw no future with Mr. Richardson, but swallowed his pride for several weeks until he could get another job. And, as he told me, the work at UPS wouldn't interfere with his schoolwork.

Two weeks later, we met at the diner in West Orange and had plenty to talk about.

"How is the work at UPS? Are you building muscles? Is it tiring? Can you stay awake in class?"

Eddie answered my questions one by one: "The work is fine and I lift about thirty to fifty pounds all the time. I don't know if I am getting stronger, but the work is pretty easy but boring. I only have classes three times a week so the work doesn't interfere with my homework. But, I get tired sometimes."

It is still hard for me to realize the change that has come over Eddie. He is so focused and mature. He is planning to buy a car and wanted to know about investing money. Part of me is so happy, but the other part is prepared for another shoe to drop.

When the check came I said to Eddie, "When you graduate and get a job, YOU are taking me out to lunch. Got that, Eddie?"

His reaction almost brought me to tears. "I can't wait for that day. You have done so much for me for so long; you won't ever have to buy a lunch again. You may not have courtside seats, but I am buying you lunch forever."

It is happening.

WHEELS

"I bought a car, Mr. Cooperman," Eddie said.

"When, and what kind?" I asked.

"A 2003 Dodge Caravan. It is in really good shape, but Jamal made fun of me for buying it."

Jamal is Eddie's good friend and he is on the police force in Newark. "Why is he putting you down, Eddie?" I asked.

"He thinks that it's an old man's car, and that I shouldn't be driving something like that. But, I like it, and it was a good deal."

I was pleased that Eddie was becoming more and more independent and responsible, but couldn't help wonder if the used car salesman hadn't taken advantage of a young man not wise in the ways of evaluating a used car. Since the purchase was already made, I commented only on the maintenance aspects.

"Do you have the owner's book in the car, Eddie?"

"I think I saw something in the glove compartment. Why?"

"Cars can cost a lot in repairs, and one way to keep them to a minimum is to do the required maintenance that the manufacturer recommends."

"That makes sense," Eddie said, "I'll read what it says."

I'm not sure he will follow this advice, but he is a man now and must accept the consequences for his decisions. I know it is hard to go against the grain of what your contemporaries think you should have. I know because I was a paper boy for several years and when I was seventeen, I bought a neighbor's 1938 Plymouth in 1952. I got a chorus of catcalls and laughter when I pulled into the high school parking lot, as many of the other cars were V8 Fords and Mercury's. So, I had some idea of how Eddie felt.

HALF FULL

Maybe it is Janine who is having such a positive influence on Eddie. Or, maybe he is just growing up and thinking more maturely. Or, maybe my pounding the message that education and hard work are keys to success has finally taken hold. Or, maybe he sees Celie working so hard, but, with a lack of a high school diploma and further training, she cannot really advance financially.

Whatever it is, I can see it in his attitude and hear it when I speak with him on the phone. Eddie now sees possibilities, where before he only saw dead ends. Although many urban students attend community colleges, four year institutions, and reputable trade schools, far too many urban young people believe that opportunities are not for them, even though the opportunities are there.

In my decade of working with disadvantaged black youth and their families, too often I saw young men reject the tried and true of study and hard work. Gangs, the lure of the street culture and the mistaken belief that doing well in school was "acting white" has doomed many young men to a life of wasted opportunities. Although Eddie didn't join a gang or hang out on the street corner, he seldom applied himself in school. The results showed, and he ultimately dropped out of school, as I related in a prior chapters.

But, now Eddie recognizes that he wasted two years and has to make up for his bad decisions. First, he got the GED, then he applied to and was accepted by DeVry. And, now he is working at UPS at the same time he is taking his coursework. But, it is his attitude that has made me a believer. Eddie thinks he can make something of his life. However, the important thing is not so much that I believe, but that Eddie believes. And he does.

I don't know why, but I thought perhaps there was a delayed reaction and he remembered the various black men we had met in the McDonald's when he was younger. Or the book which discussed the many black men and women who succeeded: businessmen, the lawyers, doctors and many other jobs that required study and perseverance. So I asked him.

"Do you remember when we were in McDonald's and I used to talk with men who were eating there? I asked them what they had to study to get their jobs and they would share their experience with us."

"I don't remember that at all. When was that, Mr. Cooperman?"

"Eddie, do you remember the book we read about famous black men and women who have succeeded as businessmen, lawyers, and doctors?"

"I sort of remember, but I can't remember a lot," he said.

It was evident now that until Eddie was ready, my efforts hadn't gotten through to him.

"I know you were trying to help me then, but most of my teachers were terrible so I couldn't see the sense of studying," Eddie said.

"Thank goodness you see now what education can do for you," I said.

"I really do; sometimes I think those guys who hang around on the corner of my street need someone to kick their rear to show them that the whole world isn't against them, but if they

HALF FULL

continue to believe that, then they probably won't ever do anything productive."

Did I hear right? Did Eddie say that?

Eddie then launched into a monologue about what he is learning at DeVry. He enjoys the computer classes and says he will teach me PowerPoint anytime I want to learn. I will take him up on his offer because I would like to learn, and also because we both understand what this will mean to our relationship. Eddie realizes now that I don't know "everything", and there are some things he knows that I don't.

Hooray!!

233

JANET

For eighteen months after Paulette died, I was not interested in seeing women socially. I had my children, grandchildren, friends, and work. That was enough. At first, I could not concentrate to read anything, but slowly I began to read newspapers. It took over a year before I could pick up a book to read. In some ways, I was like a child, doing things for the first time.

Friends asked me if I wanted to date. At first, the mere thought of being with a woman other than Paulette was distasteful to me; and I thanked them but said I was not ready. One day, about eighteen months after Paulette died, a woman, who was a superintendent in a neighboring town, called me and asked if I wanted to go to lunch. She had lost her husband a few years before, and thought since we were both educators, that conversation would be easy.

It wasn't until we were halfway through the meal, when the background music, which I had hardly heard, played "Annie's Song" by John Denver. I had told Paulette when I first heard it that I wish I could have written that for her. Quite suddenly, I had a hiatal hernia attack. I could hardly talk and managed to excuse myself to go to the men's room. It was no use, the discomfort would not go away, and I came back to the table, and said I had to leave. The past was very much with me, as it would continue to be.

A few months after this incident, I tried again. At first I felt like I was seventeen and I was uncomfortable. What was I doing here, making small talk? Why wasn't Paulette with me? Why did this have to happen? But, slowly I became more comfortable and adjusted to my circumstances. I had to come to grips with the fact that Paulette was not coming back to me. I had to live in the present.

After four years of meeting quite a few women, I met Janet. The first date was nice, but nothing really unusual. But, on the second date we had lunch and talked and talked until 7:00 PM. I knew this was not just another date.

Janet had lost her husband fifteen years before. On one of our early dates she told me that she had lived her life in reverse. She explained, "When I was married we had a lovely home, a swimming pool, and belonged to a country club. I guess I could say I lived a privileged life. But, after John died, I found his business had deteriorated due to his protracted illness, and there was no insurance. At age fifty-two I went to work full-time. I initially worked for Macy's, then Hartford Stage, and presently I am working at the Mark Twain House and Museum. I had to make all decisions myself and, to a great degree, start from scratch."

I had met some women who felt they were "entitled" and the male was to make sure they got what they wanted. This was not the type of woman I wanted to be with, and Janet's last fourteen years had made her anything but a "princess".

I found Janet to be intelligent, upbeat, and possessed with a wonderful sense of humor. And, the glass was almost always half full. We had an easy relationship and I was very comfortable with her.

During the next few months we saw each other constantly, and knew this relationship was something special. We knew this was "it," and I was able to love again. I looked forward to seeing Janet, to being with her and considering a future with her. After some time we decided to marry. Since Janet was living in a small apartment and I had a lovely home, we agreed that my home in Bernardsville would be where we lived.

Our marriage took place in Bernardsville, with only our children and grandchildren in attendance. I like Jan's children very much, and she is most comfortable with my children. Although getting along with each of the partner's kids is not a requirement for a successful marriage, it sure helps.

LUNCH

I told Janet about Eddie and his family. After meeting several times with Eddie for breakfast or lunch at a diner in West Orange, I would tell Janet what we discussed. She seemed interested and asked if she could meet Eddie at some time in the future.

"I was thinking of inviting Eddie, his mom, grandmother, and his brother, Duane, to lunch next month. If they can make it, would you like to come?" I asked.

"I sure would, Saul. You have talked about Celie with such fondness that I would like to meet her. And, Eddie, of course."

I arranged the lunch, and we drove in two cars, with Celie and Eddie's grandmother in mine while Eddie drove his car with Duane. We met at Pal's Cabin, a nice restaurant about five miles from Eddie's home, and had a wonderful lunch. Celie and Janet talked easily, and Grandmother Johnson and Janet were laughing throughout the meal. I was happy things were going so well.

On the way to Eddie's home, I noticed several police cars near his street, and, as I was about to turn into Robinson Street, I noticed it was blocked by a police cruiser. Celie was upset, as none of us knew what was going on. When I asked a cop what was happening, he gave me a "police business" reply.

"Would you like to go someplace until they remove the police car?" I asked.

"No, it's probably nothing," said Celie. "If the cops will let us walk to our home, that's what I would like to do."

We asked the police if Celie and her mom could walk the short distance to their home, and they said okay. Mrs. Johnson and Celie got out of the car and we said goodbye.

"What do you think is going on, Saul?" Janet asked.

"I have no idea, but there are three police cars, and I counted five cops in the street. There is obviously something happening that brings them to a quiet street in such numbers."

An hour later I called Eddie and asked him what that was about.

"I think there were drug dealers in a house across the street. They had a gun and the cops were trying to get them out. After a while, they came out, and the cops took them away."

Eddie said this in a matter- of-fact way. "Nothing to worry about, Mr. Cooperman, everything is fine now."

When I told Janet of our conversation, she couldn't get over that this was part of Eddie's life, his neighborhood.

The look on her face said it all before she began to speak, "You see this type of stuff on TV and read about it in the papers, but it is so different when you see where Eddie, Celie, and Duane live. It is very hard to grow up the right way when you are surrounded by this stuff."

Jan is right. It is relatively easy for a child living five miles away in Livingston, but so difficult in Newark, East Orange, or Orange.

STILL LEARNING

I'm still learning.

I talk less than I did when Eddie was younger. Then, I saw so much that needed my attention that I was quick to buy books, read with Eddie, do multiplication tables, teach him table manners, and constantly try to show the link between education and a good job.

From Eddie's viewpoint, he saw me as a ticket to New York, basketball games, the Jersey shore, McDonald's, and trips in the car to places he had never been. The link between education and "possibilities" was too far a leap for Eddie when he was younger.

When I would ask Eddie to pick out five words each week from stories he was supposed to read, look them up in the dictionary that I bought him, and use the new words in a sentence, he would not do these things at all, or would do them in a sloppy fashion. His world was not my world, and I should have done a better job of understanding his heroes, his lack of respect for learning, and the difficulty of the "role models" in his neighborhood who had the fancy cars and bling.

If I had to do it over again, I would have talked less, asked more questions, listened more, and set my initial goals lower, and kept hammering at those goals. And, the goals had to be instantly attainable; the rewards for high grades were too distant, and went counter to the norms of his peer group. This was hard for me to swallow, but doing well in school was not a positive thing; if one did well, as I mentioned before, they could be accused of "acting white." Like it or not, this was a fact of life I had to deal with.

When I picked up on Eddie's concern about people who looked at us in a strange manner, it quickly showed Eddie's views that all whites are prejudiced against blacks. When he mentioned Anne Frank, the subject of race relations came to the fore again. But, since Eddie was older, he talked more, and felt comfortable with me on this very sensitive subject.

I hadn't heard of Tupac Shakur and Biggie Smalls before I met Eddie, but I soon learned that some people Eddie looked up to were not people I held in high regard. I needed to understand the appeal of Shakur and Smalls and other people Eddie respected, and try to see things more from his viewpoint. I couldn't get close to Eddie and have the free exchange we have now if I had not tried to meet him half way by learning about the people he admired.

Initially, we talked about basketball, and Eddie was impressed at my knowledge of pro basketball. In fact, I read articles on basketball much more than usual and would bring some things to Eddie's attention that he didn't know and became "cool" in this regard. He wanted to know how I could consistently hit my jump shot from fifteen feet.

Basketball brought us together, but, if I were wiser than I initially was, I would have looked to see Eddie's frame of reference and his needs, and moved from there. I was so anxious to address so many issues that many things I tried were rejected by Eddie.

Simply bringing Eddie to our home had a profound effect on him. He saw how "big it was", and that it "had two bathrooms" and that "tigers could be in the woods", and, as I mentioned before, he chastised me saying, "Why don't you give Mrs. Cooperman a gun so she can protect herself when you are away?" Eddie wanted to know, "Who takes care of the road that comes to your house?" (the driveway) In these things, and many more, Eddie told me where *he* was, and each provided me with an opportunity to react to his thoughts or concerns. I should have sought to let Eddie establish the conversation more often, instead of my desire to always "teach".

CONCLUSIONS

What have I learned in my fourteen years with Eddie?

Primarily, how difficult it is for a child, without a father, to become a productive, caring adult. "The streets" of urban America are spoken of as if they are a living entity, as in "the streets got him". Children play on the sidewalks, watch the drug "action", the gangs, and the unforgiving culture of urban life. And they learn from this.

Without two parents, young men see their role models as the older males around them. And the models are invariably bad ones. Eddie, like any child, wanted a father's love, but was rejected by his father. Celie was trying to be both father and mother but the culture of the streets often enveloped Eddie. On several occasions when he was young, Celie would keep him home and not allow him out after school where the influence of the streets would be overwhelming. When Eddie gave me the Father's Day gift, it was, to me, on one hand, a breakthrough. I was now the primary man in his life. On the other hand, I realized I had a big responsibility to his child who was reaching out to me.

I understood, in our beginning together, that Eddie would see me as a source of entertainment. That is, after all, part of what it means to be a parent, to have a good time with your child. Eddie saw eating out, going to basketball games, and having lots of fun as his agenda, which was understandable. I learned that my objectives of "school" and "education" weren't very high on his priority list. The concept of deferred rewards was incomprehensible, especially if a kid thought he might not live to adulthood.

The values that were drummed into my head as a child were different than those formed by Eddie. I had two parents, structure, an emphasis on schooling, and a neighborhood where nobody got shot, there were no drug dealers, and my friends had upbringings much like mine. So, there were significant gaps between us, and as a result, there was a silent, but continuous tug of war between Eddie and me. If I were to do as Celie asked, and "bring Eddie up the right way," then I had to give him a chance to see a better and very different future. And, this would mean challenging him on his turf, the only playing field he knew.

I almost gave up, but, I learned that persistence, dogged persistence, would be the key ingredient if I were to succeed with Eddie. I had to see him often, let him know that I would be there for him, because, at a young age, he learned that most adults were not dependable. And, I had to keep at the values that would mold his character, because this was the be all and end all for me.

Perhaps the one thing I did that established a bond between us was simply showing up. If I said I would do it, I did it. This, I think, was the key ingredient that solidified our relationship. Only time spent with Eddie, building trust and being dependable, enabled our relationship to overcome the hurdles inherent with an older, middle class white man and a poor, young black male.

Eddie and I developed trust and friendship, which took time. And our friendship grew, as you have read, three steps forward and one step back. We had some difficult times, especially when Eddie dropped out of high school. When he spent months doing little after quitting school, Eddie had to decide if that was the life he wanted.

I would like to think my continuous "messages" had something to do with his new found resolve. Maybe Eddie realized I might not see him again and this motivated him to get the GED. Or, perhaps it was something else or a combination of factors. Whatever it was, when he got off the deck, I could see the determination in his voice and see it in his eyes. He was ready to grow up.

And grow up he has. The maturity has been evident in everything he does. Recently he told me he has been saving money and wanted to discuss how he might invest it. Eddie is twenty two and will graduate from DeVry in the fall of 2010 with an Associate Degree in Computers. He will have a marketable skill, and he will be self sufficient.

And, after the first year or two of seeing Eddie, something else was growing inside of me. Love for Eddie. Slowly but surely, friendship became caring for him, and then caring slowly moved into the emotion of love. Yes, I love Eddie very much. As I write this in the spring of 2010, I know that I will be with Eddie for the rest of my life. He is now and will be an integral part of my life. And that makes me feel very, very good.

****

If you are considering mentoring a child, I would ask that you be prepared to make at least a two-year commitment. There is nothing worse for a child than to have his or her hopes raised, and then experience what they "know," that adults will let them down sooner or later.

Why two years? Because you will be able to adjust to the child's family, and the neighborhood, and everyone will be able to adjust to you. That may not be easy. Celie was, and is, a good person, and a happy one. She is positive, strong and optimistic. She made me feel welcomed and that is not often the case, and the child is part of a family, no matter what the problems are in that family.

When I started a mentoring program in Newark, a majority of the mentors quit within a year. "I drove forty minutes to find that nobody was home, after we had made a clear date for my meeting with her child." "Things were fine until the mom kept asking me for a few dollars to pay this bill or that bill. I finally got tired of being hit upon." "The neighborhood scares me. It was okay in the summer when I started, but I was afraid to go there after dark. Too many chances I was not prepared to take." These were some of the comments of a few of the mentors who gave up early.

The difference in the mentor's life, and the life of the child and his family, was often the deal breaker. Be prepared to understand that your child's environment is very different from yours. *That's why the kids need mentors.* And, from the bottom of my heart, if you hang in there, you will get much more than you give. REALLY.

There is a Hebrew saying that if you save one life, it is as if you are saving the world. Maybe not the world, but a very good feeling that you have made a difference.

DISCUSSION QUESTIONS

Did Saul's background as a child hinder his relationship with Eddie?

Was Saul fair in comparing Eddie's room as limiting his opportunities to the fish that were bound by the confines of their tank?

Saul mentions several times that young black men didn't achieve because they would be "acting white". Do you think this is a real situation? If you answered "yes", why is it, and how do we reverse this mind set?

Eddie was astounded at the size of Saul's home. Could Saul have better used Eddie's wonder to help their relationship?

Eddie didn't remember Saul's approaching black men in the McDonald's and asking them what they had to do to succeed. What could Saul have been done better, or was Eddie to young to get these messages?

Paulette felt that Eddie was getting what he wanted but Saul wasn't getting what he wanted. Do you agree with her?

Was Saul's saying he would not see Eddie after he dropped out of school the turning point in their relationship?

**Intermedia
Publishing Group**

Publishing That Works For You

Do you need a speaker?

Do you want Saul Cooperman to speak to your group or event? Then contact Larry Davis at: (623) 337-8710 or email: ldavis@intermediapr.com or use the contact form at: www.intermediapr.com.

ABOUT THE AUTHOR

Saul Cooperman is a lifelong educator. As a teacher, high school principal, superintendent of schools and Commissioner of Education in New Jersey, the education of children has been his passion. He has served on national commissions and in the 1990's began working with troubled families in Newark, N.J. As part of his work, he created the 10,000 Mentors program.

Saul has published 67 articles in professional journals and written a book, "How Schools Really Work", a practical guide for parents. He is married and has three children.